A Problem of Fit

A Problem of Fit

*How the Complexity of College Pricing
Hurts Students—and Universities*

PHILLIP B. LEVINE

THE UNIVERSITY OF CHICAGO PRESS   CHICAGO AND LONDON

The University of Chicago Press, Chicago 60637
The University of Chicago Press, Ltd., London
© 2022 by The University of Chicago
Published 2022
Printed in the United States of America

31 30 29 28 27 26 25 24 23 22   1 2 3 4 5

ISBN-13: 978-0-226-81853-5 (cloth)
ISBN-13: 978-0-226-81855-9 (paper)
ISBN-13: 978-0-226-81854-2 (e-book)
DOI: https://doi.org/10.7208/chicago/9780226818542.001.0001

Library of Congress Cataloging-in-Publication Data

Names: Levine, Phillip B., author.
Title: A problem of fit : how the complexity of college pricing hurts students—
    and universities / Phillip B. Levine.
Other titles: How the complexity of college pricing hurts students—and universities
Description: Chicago ; London : The University of Chicago Press, 2022. |
    Includes bibliographical references and index.
Identifiers: LCCN 2021045191 | ISBN 9780226818535 (cloth) |
    ISBN 9780226818559 (paperback) | ISBN 9780226818542 (ebook)
Subjects: LCSH: College costs—United States. | Education, Higher—United States—
    Finance. | Student aid—United States.
Classification: LCC LB2342 .L477 2022 | DDC 378.3/8—dc23
LC record available at https://lccn.loc.gov/2021045191

♾ This paper meets the requirements of ANSI/NISO Z39.48-1992 (Permanence of Paper).

DEDICATED TO DAVID CARD, RON EHRENBERG, AND OLIVIA MITCHELL, MY UNDERGRADUATE AND GRADUATE ADVISERS. I WOULD NOT BE WHERE I AM TODAY PROFESSIONALLY WITHOUT THEIR INSPIRATION, GUIDANCE, AND TRAINING.

Contents

Preface

Parents often do not share their own financial information with their children, and my family was no different when I was growing up. I knew we lived in a pleasant suburb outside of Syracuse, New York (DeWitt), and we owned our own home. My father worked in the retail trade industry then. As I grew up in the 1960s and 1970s, it is not surprising that my mother's labor force attachment grew over time, but my father's salary was our dominant source of income. I also knew that my father lost his job in every recession, of which there were a few in the 1970s.

As I was approaching college age, how I was going to pay for college was a legitimate concern. My family's income clearly was not low, but college was expensive, and despite having limited information on my parents' finances, I knew they were worried about college costs.

In the end, I attended the New York State School of Industrial and Labor Relations at Cornell University, an institution to which I am deeply indebted for the education I received. As its name suggests, it is supported by the state, as are three of the seven undergraduate colleges at Cornell. If I recall correctly, the cost of attendance (COA), including room and board, was around $5,000 per year for a resident of New York State (I can confirm that the tuition alone was $2,800 in the 1981–82 academic year). That translates to around $14,000 today after accounting for inflation. In 2020–21, the full COA for a New York State resident is around $58,000; that price has risen faster than inflation, at least partly because state support has declined.

I remember my father sitting at the dining room table spending hours trying to complete the financial aid application forms. There were papers everywhere. Bad words left his mouth. When all the numbers were crunched, I qualified for subsidized student loans and some work-study funding. In retrospect, and knowing what I now know, that information provides me with an excellent understanding of my family's financial position at that time—firmly entrenched in the middle class.

In my academic career, I have devoted my attention to matters of social policy and economic disadvantage, but college costs and financial aid did not enter my research agenda until recently. I received my PhD from Princeton University and wrote my dissertation on unemployment and the unemployment insurance system. I focused on these topics through my early career research as well. My interest in these topics makes sense based on my family's experience when I was growing up. Eventually, though, I branched off and focused on an array of other topics in the broad category of "social policy." I studied a number of subjects, including abortion access, teen childbearing, retirement, the consequences of economic inequality, early childhood education, firearm access, and others, but nothing related to higher education.

I came to concentrate on financial aid not as an academic exercise but as an administrative one. In the introduction, I describe the process that led me to engage with the substantial problems in the financial aid system, brought about by my experiences with the system when my children were approaching college age. It was at that point, around 2007, that I began to investigate the idea of developing a very simple tool to estimate financial aid awards.

Soon afterward, I started working with the admissions and financial aid team at Wellesley College, where I have worked as a professor since leaving Princeton. Along with the individual training I received from members of the team, I was also the founding chair of the college's Admissions and Financial Aid Policy Committee. At the time, Wellesley College had an admissions process where faculty directly served on the Board of Admissions (separate from the Admissions and Financial Aid Policy Committee), read files, and took part in admissions decisions. I served as a member and as the faculty chair of that committee. I learned more from that role about issues in my students' lives, including the financial struggles some of them faced, than from anything else I have done in my career.

In 2013, Wellesley College launched MyinTuition, the simplified tool I created to estimate financial aid awards for students applying to Wellesley. It was successful right from the start, partially aided by the positive press coverage we received, including the *New York Times*. Not too long afterward, I started receiving inquiries from other institutions looking to replicate the tool. By that point, I understood Wellesley College's financial aid system very well, but it was unclear to me how that knowledge would translate elsewhere.

My education continued from my interactions with admissions and financial aid leaders at these other institutions. By the end of 2020, Myin-Tuition has partnered with dozens of nonprofit, four-year residential colleges and universities, including large, well-endowed, private universities and small liberal arts colleges, as well as tuition-dependent private institutions, and some public institutions. Some meet full financial need, and others do not; some also offer merit awards to a substantial share of their students. While there is always more to learn, I have been exposed to the inner workings of financial aid at a large swath of the higher-education marketplace.

Usually, an economist writing a book on a public policy topic like financial aid would conduct years of academic research and publish several papers in academic journals first. Then perhaps the individual would begin interacting with members of the policy community, communicating the results of the research and advocating for particular policies. The book would summarize what has been learned and any policy recommendations.

That is not the path I have taken. I have written policy pieces for the Brookings Institution and the Hamilton Project on college costs and pricing transparency. I also wrote a handful of opinion pieces on the topic. None of this falls into the category of traditional academic research. Only recently have I begun doing work of that nature.

I am able to write this book because of the vast knowledge I have acquired about the financial aid system from the schools and administrators I have worked with along with my broader academic training and career as a professional economist. I bring to this book an alternative perspective rather than one that is purely academic. It is informed by the practical constraints and goals of those who work in the financial aid world with the rigorous quantitative approach that economic analysis provides.

My goal in writing this book is to inform the public discussion regarding college access and the role the financial aid system contributes to it. There are obvious problems of access to college in the United States. Among the many hurdles that students from lower- and moderate-income families face are the high sticker price that colleges charge, a misunderstanding of the level of financial aid available, and the high cost that may remain even after factoring in financial aid. The lack of access combined with the substantial returns to a college investment still hinders social mobility. This is detrimental to the foundation of an equitable society.

The obvious solution is to make college cheaper, particularly for students from lower-income families. Yet that raises the question of how do we do that? This is the question I address directly in this book. A critical focus of that discussion will be the role that higher-educational institutions play in the college pricing system and how they would be affected by any changes to it. At face value, these institutions set the price. The constraints they face in doing so, though, and how they differ by type of institution, must be addressed if we are going to tackle these issues. The work that I have done with a variety of types of institutions helps inform my thoughts on this part of the problem.

Readers from different spheres of the higher-education world will benefit from this discussion. The main audience I seek to reach are those who engage in the process of setting financial aid policy. This includes both academic administrators and policy makers. Of course, this is an academic book and students focusing on the finances of higher education or economics students with an interest in social policy would find this material relevant.

On a personal note, the process of writing this book occurred during the first year of the COVID-19 pandemic. The broader crisis we faced affected all of us in personal and professional ways we never imagined. For me, the ability to sit in my (home) office and reflect on steps we can take to improve the world once we return to "normal," whatever that means going forward, was incredibly therapeutic. I am hopeful that this book will provide value to others beyond the mental health benefit it provided to me while writing it.

Introduction

My oldest son was born in 1994. I was an assistant professor at Wellesley College at the time. Two years later, I received an offer to take a one-year leave of absence from Wellesley and work as a senior economist in the White House Council of Economic Advisers (CEA). I accepted the position, and my family moved to Washington, DC, in 1996.

My portfolio at the CEA included labor market, education, and welfare policies. A big issue at that time was tax policy designed to help reduce the cost of higher education. One result was the introduction of tax-deferred college savings accounts, so-called 529 plans, which were included as part of the Small Business Job Protection Act of 1996. These plans work like individual retirement accounts (IRAs) for college.

My son was two years old then, and we had another son early the next year. I understood the benefits of 529 plans very well, so I opened accounts for each of them and started funding them immediately.

When my older son was fourteen years old, I wanted to know whether I needed to continue making those contributions. Had I already saved enough for college? As a professor, I make a good living, but not so much that paying for college would be easy. Knowing how much I needed to save required knowing how much college would cost. I wondered whether our family would be eligible for any financial aid and, if so, how much.

That is when the problem started. For current students reading this book, yes, the internet existed in 2008. Google had all the answers even then.

Well, it turns out not quite all of them. As hard as I looked, it became obvious that figuring out if my son would be eligible for financial aid was impossible. All school websites posted the "cost of attendance" (COA), a formal term that included all costs, including tuition, room and board, books, and other miscellaneous expenses. Federal law required that COA be reported. That number was often big—around $60,000 back then at many private colleges and universities.

But each school's admissions and financial aid web pages also made bold claims—"our school is affordable!" Their web sites would include a page, www.ourschool.edu/affordable. It would tell me that the school offered generous financial aid and that a large fraction of their students (50 percent? 80 percent?) received that aid. Often there would be student testimonials indicating how it would have been impossible for them to have attended the school without the help of the financial aid available.

Why are they telling me the school costs $60,000, but then telling me that a large fraction of their students do not pay that amount? What amount do they pay? Some would include statements like "The average student receiving financial aid pays $20,000" or some such figure.

If my family were eligible for financial aid, would we pay the average amount? Would we be expected to pay more or less than that amount? I wanted to know about how much *we* would have to pay.

It turned out that it was impossible to get a personalized answer to the question of how much any of these colleges would cost my family. It occurred to me that if I could not figure this out, as an economist who looks at numbers and data and dollar amounts for a living, then surely many other parents could not figure it out either.

For students from lower-income backgrounds, this would pose a far more significant impediment in their college search process. With greater financial need, understanding college costs is a more pressing issue for them. They may also have less exposure to the system of higher education, making it even more difficult for them to figure out how much college costs. Why risk searching for schools and falling in love with one or more of them without some understanding of whether it is even remotely financially feasible to attend?

New federal legislation went into effect in 2011—on account of the 2008 Higher Education Opportunity Act—mandating the use of "net price calculators" at every institution that receives federal funding for financial aid. These calculators are school-specific. They are supposed to help students understand what their cost of college would likely be after factoring in financial aid (the "net price"). The reported results are detailed estimates, not a contract fixing the price that the student really will pay. The final net price still requires filling out and submitting financial aid forms and a lengthy review process to determine an exact net price.

In practice, though, the calculators typically are not user friendly. They often use tax jargon and require inputs from tax forms. The fear and confusion that those tax forms generate is often enough to scare away potential users. They are also sometimes designed to garner prospective students' contact information to be used in a school's recruiting process as well as to provide them with an estimate of their net price. Combining those goals can turn off users who may resist identifying themselves as they enter their own private financial data. The introduction of net price calculators made it *possible* for a family to get an estimate of what a college would cost them, but it is still a difficult and anxiety-producing task.

What Is the Problem?

College as Market

This is what brought me to write this book. I am an economist, and economists understand markets. Higher education is a market, with colleges and universities representing supply and students representing demand.

But markets require prices to function well. Markets exist when there are those who want something and are willing to pay for it and others who are willing to provide it for a payment. How much of those things are produced and who gets them can be resolved by a well-functioning market with prices determining who gets what. If prices are opaque and not well understood by either side of the market, the market will not function well.

Pricing and Access in Health Care Compared to Higher Education

Economists routinely point to the market for health care in the presence of insurance as an example of a market where prices are not well known to the consumers of health care (i.e., patients). Most people have no idea how much a regular medical visit costs, since insurance pays the bill. Those with insurance may think it is a low cost, even though it is really more expensive. At little or no cost to the individual, people would be tempted to go to the doctor "too much," having a strep test conducted at the first sign of a sore throat rather than waiting a day or two as doctors recommend. In the insurance world, this is called "moral hazard." Copayments and deductibles are the insurance companies' approaches to reduce that behavior.

The market for a college education in the United States has the opposite problem. The only price that students often know is the full COA (the "sticker price"), when for most students, it is really less expensive than that. Part of the problem is that the federal government requires institutions to post that high price, and it is often the easiest number to find. In 2020, it hit $75,000 or more at some elite private institutions and $30,000 or more at public institutions for state residents. Most people cannot afford even the lower amount. At such a high perceived cost to the individual, people may be tempted to go to college "too little."

Yet most students do not pay the sticker price. The amount they pay is reduced, possibly substantially, by financial aid. What matters is the price they pay after incorporating that aid. If they do not know the amount of aid, they do not know the price. People treat health care costs as if they are less than they are and college costs as if they are more than they are. Both distort market outcomes.

Another issue that affects both the market for health care and higher education is access. In the health care sector, we worry that our current system leaves people behind. The system of providing health insurance in the United States is a complicated one, but millions of people fall through the cracks and are not covered. Uninsured and underinsured individuals face a serious risk of not being able to receive adequate care to maintain their health. Finding ways to provide access to health insurance for those individuals continues to be a major policy concern.

Access to college is an equally important issue. The return to higher education is very large, as I document in chapter 3 of this book. A college degree can raise lifetime income by hundreds of thousands of dollars.

Other research shows that a college education is strongly related to economic mobility (Chetty et al., 2020). Children who grew up in lower-income households and go on to get a college degree end up with incomes similar to those of children who grew up in higher-income households and attended the same college. Those who cannot afford to attend college do not receive those benefits.

Yet many people do not understand the financial aid available to them. They treat the sticker price as if that is what they need to pay and make college plans based on that faulty information.

Even after factoring in financial aid, though, prices may be too high for some families. Of course a family with income of $50,000 cannot afford a sticker price of, say, $70,000 at a private institution or even $30,000 at a public institution. And they would not have to pay that much. But coming up with $15,000 or $20,000 may be just as unrealistic.

A Problem of Fit

Equity is achieved in our higher-education system when all students enroll at a college that is the right fit for them. Not everyone is suited to attend college, but those who are should enroll and attend an institution where they are most likely to succeed. Some students will benefit most from attending a community college. Others are a good match at highly competitive institutions. Students should attend whichever type of institution is the best fit for them. This goal is not being met; there is a problem of fit.

Our system of higher education unfairly disadvantages children from less affluent families. Differences in educational attainment by parents' socioeconomic status (measured as a composite that includes family income along with parental education and occupations) are dramatic (McFarland et al., 2019). Among the highest socioeconomic status (SES) students (top 20 percent), 79 percent of ninth-grade students graduate from high school and enroll in college right away. For the middle quintile (40th to 60th percentiles) and bottom quintile (20th percentile or under) of the SES distribution, that figure drops to 51 percent and 32 percent, respectively.

And a sizable majority (69 percent) of the richest children (top quintile) who go on to college enroll in selective four-year institutions (McFarland et al., 2019). For middle- and lower-income high school graduates (middle quintile and bottom quintile), only 38 percent and 22 percent do so. Indeed, 61 percent of lower-income students who attend college enroll in a nonselective two-year institution (like a community college). These institutions offer important contributions in higher education, but a two-year degree is worth less than a four-year degree, and those institutions are plagued by high dropout rates (Levesque, 2018).

In some ways, it is not surprising that wealthier students have greater access to college. They have important advantages in the educational system (as well as in health care, neighborhood attributes, and other aspects of their lives) that better position them to attend college and, particularly, to attend more highly ranked colleges. Money matters in life. Those students have access to public K-12 schools that spend more money per student (Hoxby, 1998) and emphasize a college prep curriculum, have access to SAT/ACT prep courses, and have numerous other advantages that place them in a better position to attend college in ways that have nothing to do with college pricing (Lafortune, Rothstein, and Schanzenbach, 2018).

We also know that many lower-income students who navigate a more difficult path still manage to reach college age with strong academic credentials (Hoxby and Turner, 2013). Those students, though, tend to enroll in colleges that do not match their academic abilities and that have much higher dropout rates. Improving the quality of the match for these students can increase the likelihood they graduate from college and receive the tremendous returns a college degree offers. Others miss out because they choose not to attend college at all (Belley and Lochner, 2007).

Our higher-education system should ensure that students have equal access to college and that all students can attend schools that are a good academic fit for them. In the terminology of the lottery, "You can't win if you don't play." And college is far more likely to pay off than picking numbers. We need to find better ways to allow more students to "play."

Why Is This a Problem for Colleges and Universities?

Limited access to college by lower-income students harms the long-term interests of higher-educational institutions (as well as society as a whole), although the specific costs differ by the type of institution. For most institutions, the cost is in the form of declining enrollment. Diminishing birth rates since the Great Recession will result in fewer college-age students beginning in 2025 (Grawe, 2018, 2021). Elite institutions may be immune from such concerns because their national market and high demand will overcome the demographic change. For others, though, the need to maintain enrollment will become an important issue; restricting access for any groups of qualified students will not help. Now is the right time to focus on improving college access. A renewed focus on affordability and financial aid can help attract more students. Students paying less than the full sticker price still improves the bottom line when the alternative is enrolling fewer students.

Highly endowed institutions face a different issue. They have greater resources available to accomplish their mission of educating well-qualified students and can use those resources to recruit them regardless of their families' income level. Yet their students are heavily drawn from higher-income families (Leonhardt, 2017; Chetty et al., 2020). Finding ways to increase college access will better enable them to increase enrollments of well-qualified, lower-income students, ensuring that they fulfill their mission.

The Role of the Financial Aid System

It is likely that several factors prevent students from taking advantage of existing opportunities. The lack of appropriate counseling/mentoring to help make well-informed decisions is one potential problem. The complexity of the college application process is another. Any number of hurdles can interfere in the process of making decisions about one's academic future.

The financial aid system, though, is another important contributor. In fact, I believe it is one of the most significant contributors. In thinking about all the steps that need to be taken in the path of applying to and enrolling in college, the issue of affordability is often the first one. If students do not believe they can afford to attend, perhaps because it really is too expensive, it does not matter how hard the rest of the process is. They are not going. Affordability is a necessary condition.

This brings us back to prices. It is not possible to address problems associated with college access without addressing the issue of price. We must recognize both perceptions of price and actual price. The purpose of the financial aid system is to set a family's individual price of a college education. That price is different for every family other than those with incomes high enough to pay the full sticker price. For each family, the price should be understandable and known, and it should be affordable.

Most college-age students cannot afford the only price that is easily knowable, the sticker price. I show in chapter 5 that around 10 percent of college-age students in the United States can afford to pay the full sticker price of, say, $70,000 at an elite private college or university (again, in 2020). Only about one-quarter can afford to pay the full sticker price of, say, $30,000 at a four-year residential public college or university. If everyone had to pay the sticker price, we would have far fewer students attending college.

It is only because of the availability of financial aid that any students below the top rungs on the economic ladder can attend college. The scales are still tilted toward those students from higher-income families, but the inequity would be far greater without financial aid.

Yet the financial aid system needs to be more transparent and more affordable. The need to increase the transparency of college pricing—not what schools state as their sticker price but what they actually charge a family—is critical. Beyond just providing better information, though, many schools need to provide more financial aid to lower-income students.

The purpose of this book is to analyze the pricing system in higher education and discuss ways to improve financial aid to expand college access. The benefits of doing so clearly accrue to prospective college students but also to the colleges themselves.

There are three main points of fact that I document: (1) the availability of financial aid reduces the price that many students pay below, and sometimes far below, the stated COA; (2) the lack of transparency in the financial aid system prevents prospective students from understanding the actual price they would pay; and (3) even after incorporating available financial aid, the price that lower-income students are charged is beyond what they can afford at most institutions.

Why Do These Problems Exist?

The information problem, which limits understanding of what students truly need to pay, is related to institutional issues that I will address elsewhere in the book, including chapter 1. The fact that most institutions charge lower-income students "too much," though, is about economics. I examine why this pricing structure exists in the higher-education market. A better understanding of the underlying forces that drive this market outcome can help identify ways to change them.

The answers partly depend on the type of institution involved. In this book, I focus on nonprofit public and private four-year, residential colleges and universities that charge the highest sticker prices (relative to community colleges or four-year institutions with a large share of students who commute, whose stated costs do not include living expenses). Among that group, I separately consider public versus private institutions; the obvious distinction between them is the large differential in the sticker price. Public institutions also receive direct support from the state to cover some operating costs. Among private institutions, differences in the size of their endowments also matter. Some hold endowments valued at hundreds of thousands of dollars per enrolled student; funds drawn from those accounts provide extensive financial support at those institutions. Others rely almost entirely on revenues received from students to pay their bills.

The level of competition in these markets, the way that sticker prices are set, and the need to cover operating costs in a nonprofit environment contribute to the price differentials paid by students at these different types of institutions. "Competition" in this book refers to the competition across institutions for students, not the competition among students to get accepted to an institution.

The level of competition matters because it affects an institution's ability to charge different prices to different "consumers" (students). The ability to charge consumers different prices is uncommon for most products. Yet higher education (the "product") is a market that satisfies all the requirements necessary for "firms" (schools) to do so. The greater the degree of competition among schools, though, the more difficult it is to maintain wide price differentials. Ironically, higher-income students actually benefit the most from these narrow price differentials and from competition's downward pressure on prices. Simply put, it is difficult to charge them a lot more when there are more choices available.

At public institutions, pricing starts with the state setting the sticker price, with different prices set for in-state and out-of-state residents. The desire to maintain affordability, at least at face value, results in lower sticker prices for state residents. These lower prices reduce the resources available to the institutions. Combined with inadequate levels of direct state funding, these institutions have insufficient funds to provide enough financial aid to lower-income students. Higher sticker prices for out-of-state and international students help, but not enough. Real affordability is sacrificed in the name of perceived affordability at these institutions.

This problem translates to private colleges and universities without large endowments, since they face strong competition from public institutions. It prevents them from charging a lot more than what public institutions charge higher-income students, whose prices are capped by the state at relatively low levels. Their sticker prices may be considerably higher than those at public institutions, but merit aid (a topic described in detail in chapter 1) is used to lower it for many if not all of their higher-income students. This effectively reduces their sticker price and restricts revenue while also making their pricing opaque. Because these institutions also have limited endowments to draw additional financial support from, they also have insufficient funding to provide the amount of financial aid necessary to provide affordable pricing for lower-income students.

Private institutions with large endowments have the market strength and financial resources to offer much more financial aid and more affordable pricing. They face the least competition. There are fewer of them, and they distinguish themselves based on location, size, fields of study offered, and the like. MIT is not the same as Pomona College, and few students are torn between the two. The high level of demand to enroll in these institutions combined with the lower level of competition between them enables them to charge higher-income students a lot more than lower-income students. Spending from the endowment further enables these institutions to subsidize the prices charged to lower-income students.

What Can We Do to Fix These Problems?

Reducing Prices for Lower-Income Families

To solve the problem of affordability, we need to find ways to lower the cost of higher education for students from lower-income families. In terms of public policy, there are many possible approaches. The two that are discussed most frequently are to increase the size of Pell Grants and to introduce a system of "free college." The Pell Grant program already exists, providing funds to students from lower-income families to reduce the price they pay to attend college. Enhancing the generosity of those grants could accomplish the goal of making college more affordable. It also would have the benefit of improving affordability at both public and private institutions. However, this solution poses other challenges, like communicating to students how this grant and other forms of financial aid determine the final price they need to pay. Improvements to that system would be necessary as well.

"Free college" is another governmental approach to addressing the affordability issue. The general idea is to eliminate the cost of tuition at public colleges and universities. Whether such a policy would cover other expenses, like room and board, for lower-income students and whether there is an income limit that students must meet to receive free tuition depend on the specific proposal. The government would provide direct payments to public institutions to meet operating costs under such a plan. It would be a more disruptive change to the American higher-educational system, but it has the potential to accomplish the goal of making public college more affordable. The poor targeting of these funds to those who need it the most, though, is a potential problem. It also could have devastating effects on private institutions without large endowments, who would find it even more difficult to compete with public institutions that charge no tuition.

Beyond those two options, there are other ways to fix the pricing system that are less likely to be effective. For instance, states could increase their level of funding for public higher education. That money could be used to reduce the cost for lower-income students in much the same way as the federal government could do with the Pell Grant program. As I document in chapter 1, though, what we see in the data is that states that spend more on higher education use those funds to maintain lower sticker prices, which largely benefits higher-income students.

Based on the economics of the higher-education system that I previewed earlier, the most direct approach to making college more affordable, ironically, is to increase the sticker price at public institutions. That price is only paid by higher-income students. The additional revenues collected could be used to fund a reduction in the price paid by lower-income students at those institutions. It would also reduce the pricing pressure on private institutions with lower endowment values, which compete with these public institutions, and provide them with the necessary resources to reduce prices for lower-income students. The political viability of this approach, though, is limited.

Ultimately, increasing the size of the Pell Grant and free college are the most practicable approaches to make college more affordable. In chapter 6, I will provide a detailed examination of specific policy proposals to introduce these reforms and compare their strengths and weaknesses. In the end, I find the arguments in favor of doubling the size of the Pell Grant to be most compelling.

Improving Pricing Transparency    TRANSPARENCY

But making the system more affordable for lower-income students does not help if nobody knows about it. We need a better system of enabling prospective students to understand the prices they are likely to face if they attend college. Students need to know what they might expect to pay well in advance of applying to college if they are going to incorporate that into their aspirations and their decisions.

The current system clearly does not accomplish that goal. Filling out financial aid forms is no simple task. Colleges have recently adopted a "prior-prior year" policy that allows families to fill out financial aid forms based on their income from a year earlier. Families can also apply for financial aid as early as October of the year in which their child is applying to college, which is only possible if they use income information from the year before. While this policy fixes one part of the problem, it does not address the underlying complexity of the financial aid system. It just moves the fear and anxiety up by six months.

Net price calculators, mandated as of 2011, also help some, but they do not solve the problem. They are easier to complete than a financial aid form, but there is a long way to go from the complexity of a financial aid form to "easy." Evidence shows that there are substantial limitations in their implementation that reduce their value (Institute for College Access and Success, 2012; Perna, Wright-Kim, and Jong, 2019). I also document some of these problems in chapter 4. We need to do more to make college prices more transparent.

In chapter 6 of this book, I detail a proposal to redesign the process that families use to obtain information about college costs by introducing a "financial aid information funnel." Admissions officers are familiar with the concept of the funnel, starting out with a pool of prospective applicants as wide as possible and then narrowing the pool down further until a class is enrolled.

A financial aid information funnel works similarly, except the focus is cost. At an early stage of the college search process, students could access a ballpark estimate of what individual colleges might cost based on easily knowable family financial characteristics. As the process unfolds, they could provide more detailed financial information and get a better estimate. As students are applying for admission, they would complete the actual financial aid forms and, if admitted, be provided with a final price. All this information should be provided in a consistent manner across schools and over time to make it as easy as possible for students to understand.

This information funnel would benefit from other steps designed to vastly simplify the process of applying for financial aid (Dynarski and Scott-Clayton, 2007). When students submit their financial aid application, the information provided is used to determine a student's financial need and eligibility for federal financial aid. Institutions use these pieces of information as inputs in determining what they would charge students, but they do not provide the ultimate price. Legislation enacted in 2021 to simplify the FAFSA, the form required to receive federal financial aid, helps, but more work still needs to be done to better communicate that price.

Overview of the Book

The remainder of this book discusses these ideas in detail. The financial aid system and the issue of college pricing more broadly is sufficiently complex that a full understanding of these ideas requires considerable background. Chapter 1 provides an overview of the setting. How did we get to where we are? How does financial aid fit into the financial structure of a higher-educational institution? Students do not really receive a lump-sum payment called "financial aid." They receive packages of loans, work-study, and grants that reduce the price they pay. What are all those things? How is the government involved in all of this? What is the difference between need-based and merit-based financial aid? These are purely factual matters that are only well understood by those who spend considerable time in the weeds of the financial aid world. No substantive discussion of financial aid policy can occur without understanding these concepts better.

After this dive into the details of financial aid, I provide in chapter 2 a broader perspective on the college pricing system from thirty thousand feet in the air. Based on economic theory, how do we expect college prices would be set? This discussion all takes place at the level of an Econ 101: Introduction to Microeconomics course. I teach that course, and we discuss college pricing. I will discuss economic concepts of (a) price setting in markets where "firms" (schools, in this case) have the power to set their own prices; (b) game theory that describes the interaction between firms, like the prisoner's dilemma; and (c) the role of the government in the economy, including public goods and externalities. These concepts are all relevant for describing how the market for college is organized and for identifying its strengths, weaknesses, and what changes we might want to consider.

A standard approach in an economics class is to begin the analysis with a theoretical discussion, as in chapter 2, and then follow up with a presentation of data. Chapters 3 through 5 provide evidence to support the core empirical points that I highlighted above. Chapter 3 focuses on what colleges charge, both in terms of their sticker price and after factoring in financial aid. How does that differ across types of institutions and over time? This chapter also addresses a common refrain among observers of higher education—is college "worth it?" These sorts of calculations are easy to find elsewhere, but they rarely incorporate the role that financial aid plays in those calculations.

Chapter 4 addresses issues related to transparency in college pricing. Is there evidence that students are in the dark regarding the true cost of college after factoring in financial aid? If so, what impact does that have on college-going behavior? How do students respond when we undertake efforts to better communicate that true cost? I address these issues in this chapter and then turn my attention to appropriate ways to make the financial aid system more transparent.

Chapter 5 directly tackles the issue of affordability. Even if students have perfect information regarding the price of college, that price might still be too high for some of them. What does affordability mean, and how do we measure it? How does the amount they can afford compare to the amount they have to pay? How does that differ across different types of institutions? An implicit assumption in this discussion is that making college more affordable would increase enrollment. What evidence do we have indicating that lowering the price would accomplish that goal?

In chapter 6, I integrate the lessons based on economic theory from chapter 2 and the empirical evidence presented in chapters 3 through 5 to discuss the policy implications of this analysis. It is at this point that I compare specific proposals to increase the generosity of the Pell Grant and to introduce a system of free college at public institutions. I also provide greater detail regarding the creation of a financial aid information funnel to address the transparency problem.

Although transparency in college pricing and affordability are the main focuses of this book, chapter 7 will extend this analysis to focus on other constraints in the college application process that contribute to unequal outcomes by socioeconomic status. These include the complexity of the application process itself and the confusing financial aid award letters that students receive after they are accepted to an institution. Affordability must also encompass the likelihood of excessive loan burdens and an increased potential to default. The coverage of these topics is not intended to provide exhaustive analysis, but their relationship to the central issues of this book is sufficient that they require at least some discussion.

Analytical Approach and Focus

The analysis provided in this book focuses almost exclusively on the market for four-year residential higher-educational institutions. This is not intended to diminish the important role that other types of schools, and particularly community colleges, play in the college market, but the issues are somewhat different. The most obvious difference is the much lower sticker prices these other types of schools charge. At appropriate moments, I will reference that category of institutions, but it is not the focus of this book.

After imposing this restriction, I consider 1,315 higher-educational institutions with 5.8 million students enrolled, as I detail in chapter 1. Of these institutions, 456 receive public support. These public institutions are much larger on average, so they represent three-quarters (4.5 million) of total enrollment. That still leaves 1.3 million enrolled at private institutions, making them an important segment of the market to address.

I also restrict the discussion to traditional-aged college students who are living with parents (including single parents, stepparents, etc.) when they apply to college. Issues of paying for college among independent students differ from those described here. Again, this is not to lessen the importance of that segment of the market. Financing a college education for veterans, for instance, is an important policy issue, but it is one that is beyond the scope of this book.

The problems in the market for higher education that affect access are greater than those on which I will focus in this book. Much attention has been paid to the student loan crisis—the level of debt that students have taken out and the burden that places on them later in life. That issue is clearly related to what students pay to attend college. If more grant-based financial aid were offered, smaller loans would be necessary. In that sense, this book will extensively address that issue. On the other hand, the levels of debt that past students have taken out and what should be done about that are distinct topics. I present a short analysis of these issues in chapter 7, but an extensive analysis of them is beyond the scope of this book.

How much it costs to run a college is another relevant topic. Operating costs at higher-educational institutions routinely grow at a rate faster than broader measures of inflation. Why is that? That fact clearly matters here because the mostly nonprofit higher-education sector needs revenues that match its costs. If costs were lower, they could collect less. The fact that colleges have not been terribly successful in lowering operating costs reduces their ability to offer more financial aid. Other researchers have focused extensively on college operating costs, and I refer the interested reader to those sources (e.g., Archibald and Feldman, 2014). For the purposes of this book, I treat those costs as given. Providing advice to colleges to reduce those costs is also beyond the scope of this book.

This book also offers some advantages that discussions of financial aid typically overlook. First, it examines college pricing and the impact of the financial aid system on college costs for students throughout the income distribution. It is common for those who address issues of college access to focus exclusively on lower-income students. Without a doubt, those students do bear the brunt of the deficiencies of our current college payment system. Attending to the issues they face is of paramount importance.

That does not mean, though, that other students are unworthy of our attention. How well does the financial aid system address the needs of middle-class students? What about those at the top, with little financial need? Are they paying "enough"? One may have ideas about the answers to these questions, but that is not the same as evidence. In this book, I consider how much students actually pay and how that compares to what families at all levels of income can afford.

This method also has the advantage of improving our understanding of college pricing relative to frequently reported statistics. For instance, the average net price paid at higher-educational institutions is a statistic that is commonly reported. But that statistic is a function of the generosity of the institution's financial aid system and the composition of the institution's student body. One institution may have a lower average net price than another if it enrolls more lower-income students even if both would charge an individual applicant the same amount. How many lower-income students an institution enrolls is a useful statistic as well, but in terms of pricing, what we want to know is how much would the institution charge an individual student with specific financial characteristics? We cannot know this without looking at pricing across the income distribution. The analysis in this book takes that approach.

Another important feature of this book is that it assumes good intentions by higher-educational institutions. To be sure, important issues of access exist, as highlighted previously, but these issues arise despite the goals of institutions, not because of them. It is all too common to fault colleges and universities for perpetuating the inequities we observe in access to higher education. Tough (2019), for instance, claims that the American higher-educational system is "an obstacle to mobility, an instrument that reinforces the social hierarchy and prevents [lower-income students] from moving beyond the circumstances of their birth" (20). A core element of this book explores the underlying economics of the higher-education marketplace; colleges and universities may be doing the best they can given the financial constraints many of them face. Greater access to college cannot occur without recognizing those constraints and finding ways to overcome them.

I should note that much of my thinking and some of the analysis provided in this book is informed by my work running MyinTuition Corp., a nonprofit corporation (along with my position as a professor at Wellesley College). I am the founder and CEO, and after developing MyinTuition, a vastly simplified financial aid calculator initially launched at Wellesley College in 2013, I went on to develop versions for many institutions. To date, MyinTuition has contracted with dozens of colleges and universities. Since it is a nonprofit entity, I do not benefit from profits the organization generates (there are none), although I am compensated for the time I spend working on it. The experience of developing and running MyinTuition has contributed to my ability to write this book. It has enabled me to see a perspective of the financial aid system, in terms of its operation and data, to which others would not have access. I am able to view the market from the perspectives of a parent, an academic economist, and financial aid and admissions professionals.

CHAPTER ONE

The Institution of Financial Aid

The system of paying for college in the United States is not simple. Our higher-education system is decentralized, made up of independent, private colleges and universities scattered throughout the country and public colleges and universities organized at the state level. Each state system and each private institution sets their own prices. The federal government provides subsidies to students who attend these institutions, but it is not involved in setting prices. Those entities interact in the marketplace in complex ways to determine how much it will cost to attend college.

The goal of this chapter is to provide a broad overview of the institutional features that characterize the American system of financial aid. This discussion emphasizes nonprofit, four-year residential colleges, which are the focus of this book. I highlight the role played by the government along with that played by the institutions themselves in reducing how much students pay to attend college relative to the sticker price.

I start with a brief history of the financial aid system that currently exists. After that, I provide an overview of how students navigate the system and how colleges and universities determine individual student financial aid awards. Aside from the important concepts, this discussion also introduces the language of financial aid, which itself can be daunting, adding to the general confusion regarding how the system works. As a point of comparison, I also present a brief discussion about higher-educational institutions in other countries and how students elsewhere pay for college.

Since higher-educational institutions are businesses (albeit mainly not for profit; I only focus on those), I also provide a broad discussion of colleges' finances. Where does the money come from that enables nonprofit colleges and universities to pay their bills? What do they spend their money on? How does student financial aid fit into the business model of higher-education institutions?

The final section of this chapter sets up the discussion for the rest of the book by categorizing higher-educational institutions into a set of distinct markets. Aside from their academic mission, the operation of an institution like Babson College in Wellesley, Massachusetts, has very little in common with that at the University of Massachusetts at Amherst. UMass Amherst is the flagship institution in the state of Massachusetts's public university system; it enrolls twenty-two thousand students, receives $400 million from the state of Massachusetts, and charged around $30,000 in 2020–21 to students who lived on campus and received no financial aid. Babson College is an undergraduate business school with a $450 million endowment for twenty-four hundred undergraduates and a full price tag of around $75,000 in 2020–21. Yet these two institutions compete for some of the same students. In this chapter, I discuss the distinct market sectors in which institutions operate and document differences in their operations to provide background for later discussions regarding financial aid.

The History of Financial Aid

The federal government did not substantively become involved in financial aid until the 1960s, but such aid existed privately long before then (see Wilkinson, 2005, for the authoritative treatment on this topic; Fuller, 2014, provides an outstanding summary). Not long after universities sprang up in colonial America, philanthropists donated money to colleges and universities for this purpose. Harvard received its first gift, the proceeds of which were to be used to fund financial aid, in 1643. Competition is present everywhere, including among colonial philanthropists, as this initial gift led to similar gifts to William and Mary, Yale, Princeton, and the University of Pennsylvania (Thelin, 2011).

The origin of the financial aid system in the United States is partly based on philanthropy, but it also includes elements of financial aid as a pricing strategy. In the period following the Revolutionary War, the country began to expand westward, and higher-educational institutions opened in these new areas. Financial aid was necessary to attract enough students to fill them. The Louisiana Purchase in 1803 similarly led to an expansion in higher education and in financial aid.

The introduction of merit awards was tied to the introduction of the Scholastic Aptitude Test (SAT) in 1926, which was intended to identify talented, lower-income students. Although identifying meritorious students is always a challenge, test scores provide a simple mechanism to do so, even if there are limitations in following this approach. Once such a test became available, it was used for this purpose. Harvard University relied on this form of standardized testing in its introduction of the National Scholarship Plan in 1934. The Plan was designed to increase educational opportunities for highly qualified students who otherwise would not have the financial means to attend Harvard.

Just as the introduction of the SAT facilitated merit awards, the creation of a uniform methodology to determine financial need facilitated need-based financial aid. That occurred in 1954, when the College Scholarship Service (CSS) introduced a common methodology to do so. It served as a response to the different approaches that institutions were implementing to allocate need-based financial aid. It enabled students for the first time to submit a single financial aid application form and distribute it to a number of institutions. It was the precursor of the CSS Profile and Free Application for Student Aid (FAFSA) forms used today.

Almost a hundred years earlier, the federal government made its first entry into the higher-education market in 1862 in the form of the Morrill Act. The Morrill Act provided grants of land to a set of universities that served as their endowments, providing resources to fund university operations and provide greater access to college, especially in agriculture and engineering. Indeed, many of the nation's leading public universities, including UC Berkeley, Ohio State, and Texas A&M, were founded because of one of these grants. This set the stage for widely accessible institutions of higher education around the country, but it did so by providing a tremendous infusion of assets, not by directly providing financial aid to students. The educational benefits accrued from the Morrill Act are tempered by the displacement of Native Americans to acquire the land (Nash, 2019).

Some eighty years later, the post–World War II federal GI Bill (1944) provided greater educational opportunities to returning veterans. The National Defense Education Act (1958) did so as well, but, in the heart of the Cold War, its emphasis was providing trained workers to support the nation's defense. Each of these policies had the impact of broadening educational opportunities, but they were not specifically targeted at lower-income populations.

The 1960s marked the introduction of social legislation in a number of dimensions, including higher education. The Higher Education Act of 1965 established direct federal involvement in the higher-education marketplace in several ways. For the present purposes, Title IV of the law authorizes the use of federal funds to support aid for lower-income students. In 1965, that aid included guaranteed student loans and work-study support. An amendment in 1972 expanded these offerings to include the Basic Education Opportunity Grant, which was renamed the Pell Grant in 1980 in honor of Senator Claiborne Pell of Rhode Island, who sponsored the initial legislation creating these grants. Amendments to the Higher Education Act in 2008 included the requirement that institutions post net price calculators to their websites by 2011; these are intended to make it easier to understand costs at those institutions. Many of these concepts will be described in more depth later in this and subsequent chapters.

Financial Aid from the Student's Perspective

In our current world, higher-educational institutions combine available federal (and sometimes state) financial aid with their own funds to determine a level of financial aid for each student and then provide to them the result of the process (an "award"). Making those determinations is complicated. The results the institutions provide to students are complicated as well. This section will describe what students need to know to understand them. The following section will describe how institutions determine those awards.

Students just want to know how much they are going to have to pay to attend a college. A single number would be best for them. But navigating higher education's pricing system requires advanced training in the language colleges use. Both colleges and the government contribute to the confusion. I will try to clarify that language here. I have also included table 1.1, which provides a glossary that summarizes all the terms that I define here (indicated in the text with italics), which will also appear elsewhere in this book.

The number that is most easily identifiable on a college's website is the *cost of attendance* (COA). The concept was first defined in the Higher Education Amendments Act of 1972 as "tuition, fees, room and board (or expenses related to reasonable commuting), books, and an allowance for such other expenses as the Commissioner determines by regulation to be reasonably related to attendance at the institution at which the student is in attendance" (Education Amendments of 1972, 20 U.S.C. § 1070 [1973]; current version at 20 U.S.C. § 1087). In practice, there is no set method for computing the COA, and different institutions use different approaches,

TABLE I.I. Financial aid glossary

Term	Definition
Terminology Related to Student Costs	
American Opportunity Tax Credit	A federal tax credit for higher-educational expenses provided to students or their parents who attend college that is partially refundable (if no tax is owed, a direct payment of part of the available credit is made).
Cost of Attendance (COA)	The total of tuition, room and board, travel expenses, books, and other reasonable personal expenses.
Direct Subsidized Loan	Federal loans that forgive interest during the period in which the student is in school and six months after graduation. They are available for students with demonstrated financial need.
Direct Unsubsidized Loan	Federal loans that any student can borrow to pay for higher-educational expenses. Interest on these loans accrues while the student is in school.
Expected Family Contribution (EFC)	The EFC is an index number calculated from the information provided on a financial aid form that is used to determine financial need. It is a de facto estimate of the amount that a family can afford to pay for college based on their detailed financial characteristics.
Federal Direct PLUS Loan (Parent PLUS)	Federal loans that cover the cost of higher education taken out by the student's parents.
Federal Financial Aid	Financial aid that students receive that is provided by the federal government.
Federal Work-Study	A federal government program that combines federal funds and institutional funds to finance student employment designed to generate wages students can use to cover the COA.
Financial Aid Award	Combination of grants (need-based or merit-based), federal loans, and work-study expectations that helps students meet the COA.
Institutional Financial Aid	Financial aid that a higher-educational institution provides that reduces the revenue to the institution.
Institutional Grant	A need-based or merit-based grant whose cost is covered by the higher-educational institution.
Merit Aid/Award	A grant awarded to a student to reduce the COA typically based on past academic performance.
Minimum Student Contribution	The amount of funding students themselves are expected to pay based on outside income from summer employment (not work-study).
Need-Based Grant	Grant to cover COA that is based on a student's financial circumstances.
Net Price	The COA less any grant aid. It is also equal to all payments that students make to colleges regardless of form (includes out-of-pocket costs, loans, and work-study funding).
Parent Contribution	The component of the EFC that is based on the parents' finances.
Pell Grant	Federal grant available to lower- and moderate-income households to cover some of the cost of attending college.

continues

TABLE 1.1. *(continued)*

Term	Definition
Terminology Related to Student Costs	
Scholarship (Private)	A grant awarded to the student from an external source, like a private foundation or a civic organization.
Stafford Loan	Umbrella term for Direct Subsidized and Unsubsidized Loan programs.
Sticker Price	Equal to the COA (see above).
Student Aid Index (SAI)	Replacement label for the EFC beginning in July 2023.
Student Contribution	The component of the EFC that is based on the student's finances.
Tuition	The component of the cost of college that pertains directly to the education itself.
Terminology Related to Determining Financial Aid Awards	
CSS Profile	The CSS Profile is the form used to determine families' ability to pay for college based on its detailed financial characteristics and the institutional methodology.
FAFSA (Free Application for Federal Student Aid)	The FAFSA is the form used to determine families' ability to pay for college based on their detailed financial characteristics and the federal methodology.
Federal Methodology (FM)	The federal government's method of determining ability to pay based on a completed FAFSA.
Financial Need	The gap between COA and the amount a family can afford to pay (as calculated under IM or FM, and labeled EFC).
Gapping	A financial aid policy where an institution leaves a "gap" between the student's financial need and the amount of financial aid.
Institutional Methodology (IM)	The College Board's method of determining ability to pay based on a completed CSS Profile. It is typically used at private colleges and universities.
Meet Full Need	A financial aid policy where financial aid is provided equal to the level of financial need.
Need-Blind Admissions	An admissions policy where financial need is not taken into account in making admissions decisions.
Unmet Need	The gap between financial need and financial aid.
Other Terminology	
Income-Based Repayment	A loan repayment system that ties monthly payments to a share of current income.
Net Tuition Revenue	Revenue received from students after factoring in institutional grant aid.

but its intent is clear. It is a comprehensive definition of college costs, and its presentation facilitates comparisons across institutions.

The COA is also sometimes referred to as the *sticker price*. Like the analogous concept in a new car showroom, the sticker price reflects the maximum amount one would pay. It ignores the fact that car buyers and students often pay less than the sticker price. That said, it is still the easiest price to find.

Of course, many students do not pay that amount. The sticker price does not account for any form of financial aid. There are several different forms that aid may take, but I first distinguish its sources. Both the government (mainly the federal government, but some state governments provide some limited financial aid funding; I ignore the state funding in this discussion) and higher-educational institutions themselves provide financial aid. These sources are labeled *federal financial aid* and *institutional financial aid*, respectively.

From an individual student's perspective, the source of the aid does not matter. A student completes a financial aid form (or forms—more on that below) and, based on the detailed financial information provided, the institution determines how much the student will be asked to pay. If the student is eligible for aid, that amount will be less than the sticker price. Whether that difference is filled in with federal aid or institutional aid largely does not affect the student.

To elaborate on that point, consider students whose families' finances are very limited and the financial aid system determines that they cannot afford to pay anything toward their education. The students are applying to institutions that charge a $30,000 sticker price, and they receive a financial aid award that reduces the price by $20,000, leaving the student with a $10,000 bill (the fact that these students are charged more than they can afford is called a *gap*, as described below). How that $20,000 award is differentiated between federal aid and institutional aid does not change the price to students. They still need to pay $10,000. In the discussion that follows, I will elaborate on which forms of aid are provided by the government and by the institution, but both reduce the price that students pay regardless of the source.

In terms of the specific form of aid that individual students receive, the aid can take the form of grants, loans, and work-study funding. *Grants* represent the equivalent of direct reductions in the COA that do not require anything in return from the student (aside from satisfactory academic performance for continued receipt). They are the best form of aid from a student's perspective.

When a grant is awarded in recognition of the limited financial re-sources of the student's family, it is known as a *need-based grant*. When it is awarded based on the student's academic achievement or on another aspect of accomplishment (like artistic or musical ability), it is known as *merit aid* or a *merit award*.

The federal government provides need-based grants; the largest and most well-known of them is the *Pell Grant*. As indicated earlier, it pro-vides up to $6,345 in funding in 2020–21. The eligibility rules and exact formula for determining this award are described below. States also offer similar types of grants in addition to the Pell Grant; examples include the Cal Grants, Ohio College Opportunity Grants, Virginia Commonwealth Award Program, and the like. These awards are typically smaller in size than the federal Pell Grant, but they work similarly.

Another form of subsidy provided by the federal government func-tions through the tax system. The *American Opportunity Tax Credit* pro-vides a credit of up to $2,500 for students attending college, awarded to ei-ther students or their parents. Tax credits reduce the amount of tax owed dollar for dollar. This tax credit is said to be "partially refundable" in that if no tax is owed, the student or parent can receive a direct payment of $1,000 (it would be "fully refundable" if that direct payment equaled the full amount of the credit—$2,500).

Colleges themselves also offer grant funding to students, which are la-beled *institutional grants*. They can be either need-based or merit-based. They may be very large in size, depending on the institution and its COA, perhaps worth tens of thousands of dollars to the student.

Loans need to be repaid by the student. The primary federal higher-education loans for students are *Direct Subsidized Loans* and *Direct Un-subsidized Loans*, commonly referred to collectively as *Stafford loans*. The lender for these loans is the federal government, not a private bank. Subsidized loans are only available to students with *financial need*, which exists when there is a difference between the COA and the amount the family can afford to pay. The interest on subsidized loans is forgiven while the student is in school and for six months after graduation. Any student can take advantage of the unsubsidized loan program, but interest begins accruing as soon as the loan is disbursed to the student. In 2020, students can borrow up to $3,500, $4,500, and $5,500 in their freshman, sopho-more, and then junior and senior years, respectively, in subsidized loans and $2,000 in unsubsidized loans each year (students ineligible for sub-sidized loans can borrow the combined amounts in unsubsidized loans).

The federal government caps the maximum amount a student can borrow from these loan programs at $31,000 as of 2020.

Students can borrow money from other sources to pay for college as well, though. Indeed, stories in the news about students borrowing $100,000 or more for college require loans from these other sources. The federal government enables an undergraduate's parents to borrow money to pay for their child's college expenses up to the full COA less grant aid. These loans come from the *Federal Direct PLUS Loan* program (the loan is called the Parent Loan for Undergraduate Students, sometimes referred to as Parent PLUS). Beyond governmental sources, private lenders, like banks, also make available funds that students can borrow. Of course, all these loans need to be repaid. Their role is to shift the cost of college from today to later periods in life.

Importantly, these other sources of borrowing beyond Stafford loans often are not incorporated into a financial aid award calculated by the institution of higher education. Students and their parents may choose to borrow from these sources to cover the amount owed after factoring in other forms of financial aid, but these sources of funding generally are not considered financial aid by the school. Regardless of the source of the loan, loan funds are disbursed directly to the colleges.

Students taking out Stafford loans have the option of repaying them based on a percentage of their income after graduation. This system is called *income-based repayment*. The Congressional Budget Office (2020) estimates that around half of loans now in repayment use it.

Work-study funding requires work that is typically done on campus for wages that are intended to be used to pay college costs. The Federal Work-Study program provides funding for jobs for students eligible for financial aid to help pay the COA. Students offered federal work-study are not guaranteed jobs, but schools have an incentive to offer jobs to them because the federal government will cover much of the cost (Baum, 2019). Students who receive work-study funding do not see a reduction in cost from the bill they receive from the college or university. They are paid wages directly from their job and are expected to use those wages toward the costs they incur, which may be other expenses like books, personal items, or travel. This often causes confusion because the billing process does not directly incorporate this form of aid awarded. It also creates problems when students face significant difficulties finding work-study jobs, as occurred during the COVID-19 crisis (Krupnick, 2020).

A student's *financial aid award* includes grants, federal loans, and work-study for those with financial need. Students and their parents are expected to pay what remains when the total of these forms of aid are subtracted from the COA. These represent the family's out-of-pocket costs—the amount of cash they need to come up with to cover the COA. Those costs can be covered through savings, current earnings, additional loans, additional student wages beyond work-study, gifts from others (like extended family members), outside scholarships, etc.

Students can also cover these remaining costs through *private scholarships* provided by other institutions (a local bank, community organization, or the like). Colleges have nothing to do with these external awards. Sports scholarships are a topic that I will not address in this book. However, one could think of them as a form of a merit award where the merit is athletic. These scholarships contribute to a student's ability to pay and may displace some need-based financial aid the student would otherwise receive. Institutions often allow students to replace their expected federal Stafford loan contributions or perhaps their work-study expectations with these outside awards.

Recently, the concept of *net price* has received greater recognition. As highlighted earlier, since 2011, colleges have been required by the federal government to post net price calculators online that enable users to estimate it based on their individual finances. The net price is defined as the COA less grant aid. In essence, grant aid is money that never needs to be paid by the student. Both work-study and loans are the responsibility of the student, with work-study "repaid" through work during college and loans repaid through wages after graduation. As such, they represent alternative forms of costs to the student. Subtracting grant aid from the COA generates an inclusive measure of cost, which is what net price is intended to capture. Although net price is typically defined as the COA less grant aid, one should note that this is identical to the sum of students' out-of-pocket costs, loans, and work-study.

Financial Aid from the College's Perspective

How Much Can a Family Afford to Pay?

To start the financial aid process, the first thing that happens is that students complete financial aid forms. The purpose of that step is to construct a measure of how much families can afford to pay. The federal government uses that information to determine eligibility for federal financial aid (as do states if they award aid separately). Institutions use it as well to determine if they are going to provide additional aid beyond that provided by the government. Regardless of the form of financial aid, the first step in generating a financial aid award is generating an estimate of what a family can afford to pay for college (chapter 5 provides an extended discussion of these and other conceptual issues involved in determining what is affordable).

This raises the obvious question of figuring out exactly what that means. How much a family can afford is not a clear concept. One problem is the distinction between "can afford to pay" and "wants to pay." Families that understand the need to contribute to the cost of their child's education still have other uses for that money. Determining how much they can afford requires value judgments on those other uses. Families with the misfortune of suffering large medical expenses should be granted some leeway. It would be difficult to do so for families using their funds to maintain a vacation home. Of course, extensive gray areas exist between these two examples.

Identifying sources of money presents another problem. Many households have one main source of money—employment. Perhaps they have some financial wealth, but that usually comes in the form of common investment vehicles (a home, cash in a bank account, maybe some stocks and bonds). The problem is that a small slice of the population has forms of income and/or investments that are harder to count—self-employment income, profits from business ownership or a family farm, income earned overseas, trust funds, and the like. The more money available from all sources, the more the family can afford to pay. The assets of small business owners are particularly troublesome—do they belong to the family or the business?

The financial aid system attempts to incorporate all of this. It does so by making students complete the FAFSA, created and processed by the US Department of Education. Completing the FAFSA is required to receive any form of federal financial aid, like a Pell Grant or a subsidized Stafford loan. Around four hundred mostly private institutions also require students seeking financial aid to complete the CSS Profile as an alternative method of determining ability to pay. Institutions that require use of the CSS Profile also require students to complete the FAFSA because that form is required to receive federal financial aid (like Pell Grants) and institutions benefit from that source of funding.

The reason those forms are so complicated is because they seek to uncover as much detail about one's income and assets as possible, regardless of their source, and as many expenses that may be considered worthy to deduct. I will discuss attempts to simplify this process later in the book, but this is how the financial aid system is currently organized.

When a student completes a financial aid form, the responses are processed, and the result is known as the *expected family contribution* (EFC). The EFC is a key element in deciding a student's financial aid award. It determines a student's financial need, which is calculated as the COA less EFC. Institutions base their financial aid awards on a student's financial need (although most do not meet that need, as detailed below). As described in chapter 6, the EFC will be relabeled the *Student Aid Index*, or SAI, in the federal financial aid system beginning in July 2023, but the concept is the same. I will continue to use the current EFC label in this book.

Although the EFC is not formally defined as an estimate of a student's ability to pay for college, that is effectively how it used. If financial need is the gap between COA and EFC, then the EFC is a de facto estimate of how much a student's family can afford. I will relate EFC to affordability throughout this book.

The EFC is made up of a *student contribution* and a *parent contribution*, which are calculated separately based on their distinct financial circumstances. Many schools require a *minimum student contribution*, which is designed to reflect earnings from a summer job that students can use to pay a small amount of their tuition. That amount differs across schools, but $2,000 is suitable as a rough approximation. To simplify subsequent discussion (which is complicated enough), I will ignore the minimum student contribution.

The language of a "contribution" is one of the confusing aspects of financial aid. Typically, a transaction in which one party gives money to another in exchange for a service is labeled as a price. Contribution has a voluntary connotation that is misleading under the circumstances.

The underlying formula used to calculate EFC from FAFSA is called the *federal methodology* (FM) and the analogous formula from CSS Profile is called the *institutional methodology* (IM). Many aspects of the two systems are the same, including an emphasis on a family's income. Both IM and FM also ignore retirement savings, regardless of its value.

There are differences, though, between the two approaches. Perhaps the major difference between the IM and FM approach is the treatment of home equity; IM includes it, and FM does not. The question behind the different treatments in the two approaches is whether a family can afford to pay more if they own a house. It is unreasonable to expect a family to sell their house to pay for college, the reasoning goes, so FM does not include it. Homeowners in very expensive real estate markets, like San Francisco, may also have very large amounts of home equity even though they are living in reasonably modest homes. It would be unfair to penalize those families.

Alternatively, home ownership represents command over greater financial resources. If one family chooses to live in a bigger home rather than invest in stocks, what is the difference in their ability to pay? The family would also have access to home equity loans that are available at lower interest rates than other conventional loans. Ignoring home equity also enables families to use other forms of savings to pay off some of their mortgage and reduce their college cost. Whether home equity should be included in determining ability to pay is far from clear. Some schools that use IM compromise and count home equity up to some ratio (for example, twice or three times) of family income.

Treatment of family structure is another important distinction between the two approaches. The concept of ability to pay is less complicated (relatively speaking) when a student's parents are married, and all their resources are considered collectively. Divorce obscures this. It may be the case that both parents recognize their responsibility toward their child and contribute to college education expenses according to their ability to pay. Sometimes, though, that does not happen. Even when it does, the situation is complicated for divorced parents who have started new families—whose resources are whose in the new family? The stepparent should not be held financially responsible, for instance. FM just ignores this issue and only collects financial information for the student's custodial parent (the one the student lives with). IM requests information from the custodial and noncustodial parent, and institutions using IM expect payment from both of them. They often consider requests to waive that expectation, though, for students who have limited contact with their noncustodial parent.

There are other differences between IM and FM, but these two clarify the issue that affordability is not a simple concept to measure. Complexities like this also illustrate why financial aid forms are so complicated in the first place. How much a family can afford seems like a straightforward idea, but operationalizing it is extremely difficult. Although calculating EFC is intended to represent ability to pay, how well it accomplishes that goal is an open question. This is an issue to which I will return in chapter 5.

How a Financial Aid Award Is Determined

Both federal financial aid and institutional financial aid use the EFC to determine the amount of aid available. Eligibility for a Pell Grant is based on the difference between the maximum award available, which was $6,345 in 2020–21, and a family's EFC obtained from FAFSA. A family that is determined to have a zero EFC receives the maximum award and a family with a $3,000 EFC is eligible for a Pell Grant of $3,345.

But many institutions offer grant-based financial aid awarded on the basis of need that goes beyond what is available from a Pell Grant. For them, the next critical step in calculating a financial aid award is determining financial need. Again, that is calculated as the gap between the COA and the amount the family can afford to pay. The Pell Grant would be applied toward meeting that financial need, but at any institution with a price tag even in the $30,000 range, some need will remain for many families. Federal loans and work-study funding along with the Pell Grant will not cover the full COA. Institutions may choose to offer additional aid beyond these sources. They may also choose to provide aid to students whose financial resources are sufficient to make them ineligible for a Pell Grant. For instance, a student whose EFC is $10,000 is not eligible for a Pell Grant, but they still cannot afford, say, $30,000 in college costs.

From here, an important distinction across schools is whether they *meet full need*. Schools that do so provide financial aid equal to the student's financial need. Relatively few institutions do so; a list of them is provided in table 1.2. There is some wiggle room, though, in defining whether institutions meet full need since they have some discretion in determining need. Two institutions that both claim to meet full need may still charge the same student different prices. Most institutions that meet full need rely on the IM as the core of its need determination process.

Other schools leave a "gap" between financial need and financial aid. This is called *gapping*; the gap is labeled *unmet need*. Most schools gap, including most public institutions.

Note that only a subset of schools that meet full need also have a *need-blind admissions* policy, meaning they do not take financial need into account in making admissions decisions. Those that are not need blind but meet full need may not accept an otherwise admissible student with financial need because of that need. If they do admit the student, though, they will provide financial resources to meet that need.

TABLE 1.2 Higher-educational institutions that meet full financial need, fall 2019

Institution	Endowment (in $millions)	Total Enrollment	Endowment/Student (in $1,000s)
Amherst College	$2,378	1,855	$1,282
Babson College*	$316	1,832	$172
Barnard College	$422	3,078	$137
Bates College	$345	2,536	$136
Boston College	$2,516	13,762	$183
Bowdoin College	$1,628	1,826	$892
Brown University	$3,604	9,884	$365
Bryn Mawr College	$897	1,654	$542
California Institute of Technology	$2,907	2,233	$1,302
Carleton College	$878	2,085	$421
Case Western Reserve University	$1,887	11,133	$169
Claremont McKenna College	$835	1,325	$630
Colby College	$828	2,000	$414
Colgate University	$924	2,954	$313
College of the Holy Cross	$783	2,923	$268
Colorado College	$765	2,121	$361
Columbia University	$10,869	27,990	$388
Connecticut College	$315	1,816	$174
Cornell University	$6,871	23,538	$292
Dartmouth College	$5,494	6,489	$847
Davidson College	$815	1,843	$442
Denison University	$850	2,376	$358
Dickinson College*	$438	2,376	$184
Duke University	$8,525	16,046	$531
Emory University	$7,985	13,498	$592
Franklin & Marshall College	$387	2,297	$168
Franklin W. Olin College of Engineering	$384	363	$1,058
Georgetown University	$1,770	16,451	$108
Grinnell College	$1,992	1,694	$1,176
Hamilton College	$1,013	1,996	$507
Harvard University	$39,234	25,070	$1,565
Harvey Mudd College	$317	893	$355
Haverford College	$519	1,309	$396
Johns Hopkins University	$4,191	19,019	$220
Kenyon College	$414	1,725	$240
Lafayette College	$871	2,618	$333
Macalester College	$771	2,153	$358
Marietta College*	$85	1,093	$78
Massachusetts Institute of Technology	$16,400	11,468	$1,430
Middlebury College	$1,124	2,574	$437
Mount Holyoke College	$778	2,248	$346

continues

TABLE I.2 (*continued*)

Institution	Endowment (in $millions)	Total Enrollment	Endowment/Student (in $1,000s)
Northeastern University	$848	21,107	$40
Oberlin College	$947	2,796	$339
Occidental College	$434	1,916	$227
Pitzer College	$141	1,059	$134
Pomona College	$2,274	1,564	$1,454
Princeton University	$25,438	8,309	$3,062
Reed College	$582	1,472	$395
Rice University	$6,229	6,903	$902
Scripps College	$362	1,066	$340
Skidmore College*	$379	2,596	$146
Smith College	$1,875	2,882	$651
Stanford University	$26,465	16,733	$1,582
St. Olaf College*	$537	3,033	$177
Swarthmore College	$2,116	1,556	$1,360
Thomas Aquinas College	$24	407	$59
Trinity College	$621	2,162	$287
Tufts University*	$1,846	11,051	$167
Union College	$457	2,196	$208
University of Chicago	$7,009	15,744	$445
U. of North Carolina at Chapel Hill	$3,308	26,978	$123
University of Notre Dame	$11,065	12,432	$890
University of Pennsylvania	$13,777	23,463	$587
University of Richmond	$2,512	3,663	$686
University of Southern California	$5,544	43,389	$128
University of Virginia	$6,856	23,312	$294
Vanderbilt University	$4,608	12,232	$377
Vassar College	$1,083	2,447	$443
Wake Forest University	$1,329	8,080	$165
Washington and Lee University	$1,603	2,221	$722
Washington University in St. Louis	$7,687	14,574	$527
Wellesley College	$2,105	2,447	$860
Wesleyan University	$1,065	3,116	$342
Williams College	$2,626	2,117	$1,241
Yale University	$29,445	13,353	$2,205

Source: Mulhere (2019) and IPEDS Data Center.
Note: Endowment values are from June 2018. Enrollments represent full-time-equivalent students, including both graduate and undergraduate students.
*Institutions guarantee to meet full need in the student's freshman year.

Schools that meet full need can do so using any or all forms of financial aid available to them. Most schools expect students to take out loans to meet some of the need, although these expectations are generally capped at either $3,500 or $5,500 in a student's first year, the loan limits just on subsidized federal loans or the sum of limits on subsidized and unsubsidized federal loans, respectively. Virtually all schools include work-study funds in their financial aid awards. Those funds usually fall into the range of $2,500 to $3,000 per year.

Combining these elements, a school that meets full need may still charge a family with $0 EFC (very low income and assets) a net price considerably more than $0, perhaps upwards of $8,000 in their first year. That amount is expected to come from a loan (up to $5,500) and wages from a work-study job (perhaps $2,500). This family would not be expected to make any cash payments toward their child's education at these institutions.

The remainder of the financial aid award at schools that meet full need is grant aid. That would include federal awards like Pell Grants, but it would mostly constitute institutional grant aid (these forms of grant aid would be listed separately on a student's financial aid award letter). The school would need to provide as much of this form of aid as necessary to fill the remaining gap between the COA and ability to pay after also subtracting loans, work-study funds offered, and federal grant aid (like a Pell Grant). Based on the assumed values here, a family with $0 EFC would receive a Pell Grant of $6,345, a $5,500 federal loan, and $2,500 in federal work-study funds. An institution that meets full need and charges $30,000 per year would then provide this family with grant aid of $15,655 (equal to $30,000 − $6,345 − $5,500 − $2,500).

For an individual family with financial need, note that the net price may differ even across meet-full-need schools because net price only subtracts grant aid from the COA. The greater extent to which loans and work-study are included in the financial aid package, the higher the net price, even across schools that meet full need. To continue with the previous example, the net price of a $0 EFC student at one of the fourteen institutions that does not include loan expectations in their financial aid awards (as of 2020; Powell and Kerr, 2020) typically would be more like $2,500 per year, which represents the amount of work-study funding offered. The entire $5,500 federal loan would be replaced with grant aid at these institutions.

The process of awarding aid at schools that do not meet full need also starts from the EFC. It then incorporates other forms of aid (Pell Grants, loans, and work-study) to determine remaining financial need, and then uses this to calculate a need-based financial aid award. The institution has full discretion over how much additional aid to award. These institutions have revenue goals they need to hit to balance their books for the year, and that affects how much need-based financial aid they can award. Note that institutions that meet full need but are not need blind also have revenue goals. They meet them based on who they admit, not how generous the aid packages are.

Some schools also offer merit awards as part of their financial aid packages. This is more commonly true among schools that do not meet full need, and those schools are more likely to offer it to a larger share of their students. Merit awards and need-based financial aid are not determined independently, though. Schools typically reduce financial aid awards, at least to some extent, to compensate for the additional merit funding they offer.

Sample Financial Aid Awards

To put some of these extensive details into more perspective, I have prepared sample financial aid awards at different types of institutions for an individual family. They are presented in table 1.3. Institution 1 meets full need. Neither Institutions 2 nor 3 meet full need, but Institution 3 offers merit aid and Institution 2 does not. At all institutions, I have arbitrarily set the COA at $50,000. The family in question has an EFC calculated to be $5,000 based on their detailed financial characteristics. Roughly speaking, this is a typical family with an income of $50,000 (see chapter 3 for more about this calculation). The difference between these two values indicates that the family's level of financial need is $45,000.

The first form of financial aid that begins to fill that gap is a Pell Grant. With a maximum Pell Grant value of $6,345 and an EFC of $5,000, the family is eligible for a $1,345 Pell Grant, which I have rounded to $1,000 in these calculations for simplicity. This amount addresses little of the family's financial need. Other forms of federal financial aid are available as well, including loans and work-study. I assume that each institution includes a loan expectation of $5,500, the maximum federal loan one can borrow as a freshman. Students may also be expected to obtain a work-study job that will provide wages of $2,500 to cover their college costs. So far, federal financial aid has covered $9,000 of the $45,000 in financial need, with $36,000 remaining.

At the next stage, the difference between institutions that meet full need and those that do not becomes apparent. To meet the remaining need of $36,000, the institution would provide that student with a grant equal to that amount. The student's net price would be $13,000, of which

TABLE 1.3 Hypothetical awards under different financial aid systems

School Characteristics	Institution 1 (Meets Full Need)	Institution 2 (Neither)	Institution 3 (Offers Merit)
Cost of Attendance (COA)	**$50,000**	**$50,000**	**$50,000**
Meets Full Need	Yes	No	No
Offers Merit	No	No	Yes
Family Characteristics			
Expected Family Contribution	$5,000	$5,000	$5,000
Financial Need	**$45,000**	**$45,000**	**$45,000**
Federal Financial Aid			
Federal Pell Grant	$1,000	$1,000	$1,000
Federal Loan	$5,500	$5,500	$5,500
Work-Study	$2,500	$2,500	$2,500
Remaining Need	**$36,000**	**$36,000**	**$36,000**
Institutional Financial Aid			
Institutional Need-Based Grant	$36,000	$31,000	$21,000
Merit Award	$0	$0	$10,000
Unmet Need ("Gap")	**$0**	**$5,000**	**$5,000**
Actual Cost to Family			
Net Price[1]	$13,000	$18,000	$18,000
Out-of-Pocket Cost[2]	$5,000	$10,000	$10,000

[1] The net price can be calculated as COA – grants or EFC + loans + work-study + unmet need. Both methods provide the same value.
[2] The out-of-pocket cost to the family is the sum of the EFC and unmet need. It is the component of net price that is not expected to be paid through a loan or work-study.

$5,000 would represent out-of-pocket costs (the $5,000 EFC), and the re-mainder represents a loan and work-study.

The major difference between that award and the awards offered by the institutions that do not meet full need is the level of grant aid. Of the $36,000 in remaining need after accounting for the EFC and federal sources of aid, these institutions would not cover all of the remaining gap. At Institution 2, which offers no merit aid, I assume that the institution provides a grant of $31,000, leaving a gap of $5,000. That amount rep-resents financial need that goes unmet by the financial aid system. This results in a net price of $18,000, of which $10,000 represents out-of-pocket costs (the $5,000 EFC plus the $5,000 gap).

Institution 3 offers merit aid. Suppose this student is sufficiently strong academically that $10,000 is awarded in the form of merit. Institutions that award merit aid typically reduce their own need-based grant in lieu of the merit offered. The reduction in institutional need-based grant aid may not be dollar-for-dollar with the merit aid, but I will assume so here for simplicity (the rate of substitution is typically very high, though). Accordingly, the need-based component of institutional grant aid drops to $21,000 in this example, leaving the same amount of unmet need ($5,000) faced at Institution 2. The merit award has an important marketing advantage, but it may not have much of a financial one for students who have financial need.

Paying for College in Other Countries

There are alternative ways that a college education is financed in different countries. Johnstone and Marcucci (2010) provide an outstanding treatment of these international comparisons that informs the discussion here.

High-income countries typically fit within three main types of financing systems. In the first type of system, tuition and fees are charged right away, payable at the point of matriculation. It is often paid by the student's parents based on assumption of parental contribution. Financial aid is available to reduce the cost for students from lower-income families. Other than the United States, Japan is an example of a country that uses a similar model to pay for college in a largely private system.

A second approach is based on deferred payments, or loans. Universities charge tuition, but students can take out loans to cover the full cost, which they repay after graduation contingent on their income. No payments need to be made while the student is enrolled. If the income-contingent payments made following graduation do not cover the full amount of the loan by the end of the loan period, the student is no longer responsible for them. Australia and the United Kingdom are countries that uses a system like this. The cost of attending institutions in these countries are roughly at the level of public institutions in the United States, restraining the amount borrowed.

In a third approach, the government charges little or no tuition; the costs of higher education are paid directly from tax revenue. Germany and France use this approach. Students still need to pay for their living expenses, although financial aid, including loans, is available to help cover those costs.

These differing systems illustrate the range of alternatives that have been discussed in the United States. The first system is the one that we currently use. The Australian model represents a substantial expansion of the system of the income-based repayment option that is already in place in the United States. The French and German models are more closely aligned with current proposals for "free college." A thorough evaluation of proposals to incorporate aspects of these other systems would be warranted before moving forward with one of them. In this book, I will discuss these policies (particularly free college because of its closer connection to pricing) in more detail later in subsequent chapters, but a careful review of the experiences in these other countries is beyond the scope of this book. Johnstone (2016) considers these issues.

Where Does the Money Come From and Where Does It Go?

A financial aid policy that meets full need clearly has desirable attributes from the student's perspective. Why do so few colleges have this policy? As much as we do not like to think about colleges as businesses, at the end of the day, they are. Just like any other business, they have revenues and expenses. They are nonprofit organizations (at least the ones I focus on here), so maximizing the difference between revenues and expenses (that is, profits) is not the goal. They do need to pay their bills, though, so revenues must match expenses. Enrolling students that pay little or no tuition makes that more difficult. The money must come from somewhere. No discussion of financial aid policy can be complete without a better understanding of how this math all works; this section covers that topic.

Sources of Revenue

The appropriate place to consider the role of financial aid in a college's budget is revenue from students. The relevant concept here is *net tuition revenue*, which captures the revenue that students pay after factoring in institutional grant aid. It is similar to the student's combined net price in capturing everything the student pays to the institution, including loans and work-study. It also includes federal sources of financial aid, though, like the Pell Grant, which reduce net price, but still gets paid out to the institution.

Revenue from students is often insufficient to cover the entire operating costs of an institution. Likely sources of additional funds to close the gap include spending from the endowment at private (and some public) institutions and state support at public institutions. Gifts operate similarly to endowment spending, and I do not address them separately. The other major revenue category (project grants and contracts) is targeted at the specific task proposed, making it difficult to use those funds for broader institutional purposes.

Endowments represent the accumulation of past large donations to an institution. Particularly at those elite institutions that have been in existence for decades (centuries?), those endowments may be quite large. Harvard has the largest endowment, valued at $40.9 billion as of 2019; over one hundred institutions have endowments valued at greater than $1 billion (NACUBO-TIAA, 2020). Higher-educational institutions with endowments have spending policies that dictate how much of those endowment funds are released to contribute to the annual budget. Although those rules can be complicated, one could approximate them with a simple annual spending rate of, say, 4.5 percent, which is consistent with the evidence provided in NACUBO-TIAA (2020). In 2019, for instance, Harvard withdrew $1.9 billion from its endowment to fund university operations (4.64 percent). Of course, Harvard is an extreme case. Most private institutions have endowments far smaller than that (although a few public institutions also have large endowments, as described below).

The availability of endowment funds enables an institution to spend more than they would if they only had revenue from students. It is easier for them to offer more generous financial aid because they have this additional resource.

Indeed, that is how schools behave. Table 1.2 details the endowment values of all colleges and universities that meet full financial need, as highlighted earlier in this chapter. Although there is considerable variability in the specific level of their endowments per student across these schools, on average this is a very wealthy group of institutions. The average endowment value per student is $556,000. If they spent 4.5 percent of that per year, it represents annual revenue of around $25,000 per student. Across 856 private colleges and universities that do not meet full need and with a "Carnegie Classification" (a system of categorizing colleges and universities in the United States by degrees offered and other characteristics) of bachelors-degree granting or higher, the average endowment per student is $85,500. At the same spending rate, those funds generate $3,800 per student. Clearly, the latter schools are going to need to be more reliant on revenues from students.

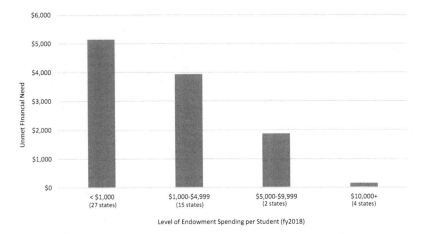

FIGURE 1.1. Fall 2019 unmet financial need at public flagship institutions: families with $50,000 in income and no assets, by endowment spending per student

Source: Author's calculations based on data from IPEDS and Levine, Ma, and Russell (2020). Only forty-eight states are included here because Pennsylvania and Wyoming are dropped from their analysis due to data limitations.

Note: All calculations are based on students with an SAT/ACT score at the 75th percentile of each institution's test-score distribution.

Public institutions typically do not have large endowments, but there is still some variation across states in their endowment values, mainly at the state flagship institutions. Here, I examine the tendency of these public flagships to use their endowments to provide more generous financial aid. I start with data from the Integrated Postsecondary Education Data System (IPEDS) on endowments per student at these public flagships. Then I add net price data for state residents with family incomes of $50,000 and no assets, obtained from each institution's net price calculator. Levine, Ma, and Russell (2020) use these data to report the level of unmet need for a student with these financial characteristics at each institution.

The results of this analysis are reported in figure 1.1. Flagship universities are aggregated into categories by their level of endowment spending per student. The top category includes schools that spend more than $10,000 per student per year—four schools are included in this category (Universities of Virginia, North Carolina, Michigan, and Texas). Three of these institutions meet full need (Virginia, North Carolina, and, for state residents, Michigan). Unmet need is very low across these four schools, representing just the small level of unmet need at Texas—$590. The less well-endowed schools, though, have much greater levels of unmet need.

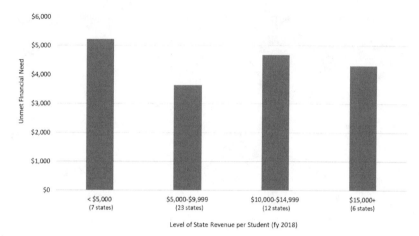

FIGURE 1.2. Fall 2019 unmet financial need at public flagship institutions: families with $50,000 in income and no assets, by state revenue per student

Source: Author's calculations based on data from IPEDS and Levine, Ma, and Russell (2020).

Note: All calculations are based on students with an SAT/ACT score at the 75th percentile of each institution's test-score distribution.

Among the twenty-seven states whose flagship institutions have endowment values per student of less than $1,000, families with those financial characteristics face over $5,000 of unmet need.

Since large-endowment values are uncommon at these institutions, perhaps state expenditures fill in part of the gap in students' financial need. Direct funding from the state to public institutions could be used to provide additional need-based aid (some states also offer direct need-based grant programs similar to the Pell Grant, although considerably smaller in magnitude).

It turns out, however, that does not happen. To examine this, I use the same measure of unmet need and divide state flagships according to the level of revenue per student provided by the state. There is considerable variation across states in revenue per student received from the state, with Oregon, Vermont, and New Hampshire receiving around $3,000 per student compared to the University of Connecticut, which receives about $23,000 per student.

The patterns across states in the level of generosity of their financial aid systems, though, appear to be weakly correlated with the level of state funding. As shown in figure 1.2, states that receive the most funding per student (greater than $15,000 per student per year) offer financial aid packages that include perhaps slightly lower levels of unmet need. In general, unmet need across states is in the vicinity of $4,000 to $5,000 regardless of state funding. The substantial additional funding that some public flagships receive is not generally used to provide more generous financial aid.

There is evidence, however, that they use this funding to keep tuition low (Chakrabarti, Gorton, and Lovenheim, 2020). Figure 1.3 is analogous to figure 1.2, except that it measures stated levels of tuition as well as the remaining student charges (room and board, etc.) for the same categories of states. It shows that flagships that receive greater state funding per student charge lower rates of tuition. Moving from the states receiving less than $5,000 in state aid per student to greater than $15,000 in state aid is correlated with almost a $5,000 reduction in the level of tuition. Differences in other student charges are trivial across these states.

This finding highlights an important point that I will address at length later in this book. Tuition rates at public institutions are typically set by state government or the state board of higher education (Zinth and Smith, 2012), not by the higher-educational institution itself. The goal of maintaining an affordable higher-education system is often viewed as keeping tuition low. Other student charges, like room and board, are typically set

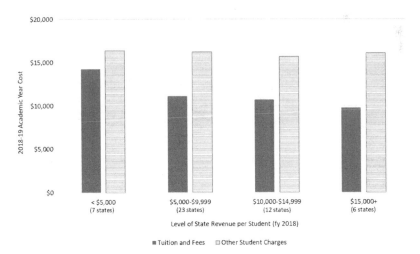

FIGURE 1.3. Tuition and other charges at public flagship institutions, by state revenue per student

Source: Author's calculations based on data from IPEDS.

at the level of the institution, so it is not surprising that state funding is unrelated to them.

According to these data, though, keeping tuition low is likely to help those with greater financial resources, but not those with weaker finances. The greater state aid required to keep tuition lower has little or no impact on reducing unmet need among students who have less money. Those who would pay full price, students from wealthy families, pay lower prices when tuition is lower. Spending more from the state to keep tuition low without helping those in the greatest financial need is an odd policy. It contradicts the goal of enabling students from all financial backgrounds to obtain the benefits of a college education.

Operating Costs

Because colleges and universities operate as nonprofit organizations (at least the ones I consider), costs need to match revenues. If operating costs rise, revenues need to rise in lockstep. If not, cost-cutting measures must be taken to maintain balance. In terms of financial aid, if revenue needs are greater because of rising costs, an institution may need greater net tuition revenue to pay the bills. That usually means less financial aid.

Historically, this was a problem because colleges and universities were consistently increasing levels of spending beyond the rate of inflation. Hinrichs (2016) presents detailed data on spending patterns by different types of institutions between 1987 and 2013. Throughout much of this period, one can see clear evidence of increased spending across the board, including instructional spending, research, student services, and academic support.

Archibald and Feldman (2014) provide three related explanations for why this occurred. First, advancing technology helps reduce costs in many industries, but higher education is not the type of industry that can benefit much from these improvements. What we do on campus today is not much different than decades ago (ignoring the 2020–21 COVID-19 experience). Second, technological progress requires a more skilled workforce, driving up wages for those skills. Those are also the types of workers that are employed in higher education, leading to rising labor costs. Third, as technology advances, colleges and universities need to invest resources to keep pace, so that students are trained in the latest methods. All these factors support rising costs in higher education.

In the recent past, these cost increases subsided, at least for a while. The data reported in Hinrichs (2016) and Desrochers and Hurlburt

(2016) show that the Great Recession appears to have ended that upward trend, at least through 2013, the latest year for which their data are available. More recent data suggest that costs have begun to rise again (Snyder, de Bray, and Dillow, 2019). The need to keep pace with technology, expand the curriculum to cover more and newer fields, and the provision of more mental health services and other support services to meet growing student needs have contributed to this increase. As I show in chapter 3, though, this recent increase in costs has not contributed to dramatically rising net prices paid by students.

Financial Models at Different Types of Institutions

As highlighted in the preceding discussion, different types of institutions operate differently in terms of their financial models. The ability to draw funds from a large endowment or the receipt of funds from state governments, for instance, has a meaningful impact on how institutions operate. This section will distinguish institutions by type, clarify their differences, and compare their finances in a more detailed manner.

I undertake this task using IPEDS data, which contain information for 6,857 higher-educational institutions in the United States. I focused on a subset of 2,107 of them. These include the 1,315 four-year public and private institutions that award a bachelor's degree or higher and are "residential" in nature (defined as having at least enough dorm capacity to house one-quarter of its undergraduate enrollment) and 792 two-year public institutions that award an associate's degree and that are nonresidential in nature (i.e., community colleges). In both cases, institutions with fewer than five hundred students have been excluded. My focus in this book is on four-year residential institutions, but the two-year institutions represent a large and important segment of the market, and I include them here for comparison purposes.

In this analysis, I also separate four-year public and four-year private institutions (all nonprofit) into two groups, each based on common characteristics. I split four-year public institutions into those that are state flagships (like UC Berkeley) and other public institutions that satisfy the Carnegie Classification of "R1" (very high research activity, like UCLA) from other public institutions (like Cal State Fullerton, classified as "R3," a doctoral university with moderate research activity). Among private four-year institutions, I split those that have "large" endowments (defined as an endowment per full-time-equivalent student greater than $150,000) from other private institutions with smaller endowments. I chose that dividing line to create a subcategory of private institutions of roughly the same size as the public flagship/R1 subcategory among public institutions.

Table 1.4 provides median characteristics of the schools within each category, focusing on admissions and financial aid, to illustrate their differences. There are substantial differences across institutions. Public institutions enroll more undergraduate students than private institutions; public flagship/R1 institutions enroll many more undergraduates. Private institutions with large endowments are more selective, admitting fewer applicants. Their students have considerably higher standardized test scores, and they are much more likely to graduate on time. Admissions statistics for the other types of four-year institutions are generally comparable to one another. Public two-year institutions are much different, with a particularly noteworthy discrepancy in graduation rates. This is a well-known issue (Levesque, 2018).

The COA (i.e., the sticker price) and financial aid profiles of these institutions are also very different. Private four-year institutions with a large endowment have a sticker price that is a lot higher than the others (all dollar values are rounded to hundreds throughout the analysis for simplicity). The entire difference is attributable to tuition and fees; other expenses, including room and board, are similar across institutions (except for community colleges, since they are not residential).

Fewer students at the private four-year institutions with large endowments receive financial aid, and they pay more, on average, even after factoring in financial aid. The problem with these comparisons, though, is that it is unclear from them whether these differences in financial aid reflect the characteristics of the financial aid system or the incomes of the students who attend. For instance, it is the private four-year institutions with large endowments that are more likely to meet full financial need. If their students end up paying more, it must be because they can afford more, according to the EFC calculation described earlier. As I document in chapter 3, these institutions charge the lowest net price to lower-income students.

Also note that the median private four-year institution with smaller endowments provides grant-based financial aid to virtually all its students. The frequency of merit-based awards at these institutions explains that; not all their students have financial need. This makes the full COA an irrelevant statistic, since few students pay that amount. Charging a high

TABLE 1.4. Admissions and financial aid profiles for fiscal 2018 by type of institution[1]

	4-Year Institutions				
	Public Flagship/R1	Other Public	High-Endowment Private	Other Private	Public 2-Year
Number of Institutions	97	359	101	758	792
Undergraduate Enrollment	23,515	5,518	2,171	1,690	4,527
			Admissions		
% Applicants Admitted	69%	75%	30%	68%	67%
% Admitted Enrolling (Yield)	31%	30%	32%	21%	49%
4-Year Graduation Rate[2]	49%	26%	82%	46%	12%
6-Year Graduation Rate[2]	72%	48%	88%	58%	26%
25th Percentile SAT Scores[3]	1,130	974	1,320	1,013	801
75th Percentile SAT Scores[3]	1,359	1,170	1,500	1,205	974
			Stated Costs (Sticker Prices)		
Median Cost of Attendance[4]	$27,100	$23,600	$70,900	$47,000	$9,700
Median Tuition and Fees	$11,000	$8,700	$52,600	$32,100	$4,200
Median Other Expenses	$16,100	$14,900	$18,300	$14,800	$5,500
			Financial Aid		
% Freshmen Pell Grants	25%	43%	17%	38%	55%
% Freshmen Any Grant Aid	74%	84%	63%	99%	73%
% Freshmen Any Fin. Aid	85%	93%	74%	100%	81%
Average Freshman Net Price	$15,900	$14,000	$26,800	$23,200	$7,000
Average Freshman Net Price: Family Income > $110,000	$22,700	$19,200	$41,000	$27,100	$11,600

Source: Author's calculations based on data from IPEDS.

[1] All statistics represent median values across institutions within categories (rounded to the nearest $100 for dollar values). All categories except for public two-year institutions are restricted to institutions where dorm capacity is at least 25 percent of the undergraduate population (i.e., "residential"). Two-year institutions are restricted to nonresidential.

[2] For two-year public institutions, the reported statistics represent the two-year and three-year graduation rates.

[3] SAT scores are combined math and reading. For institutions where more students take the ACT rather than the SAT, the reported statistic is the SAT equivalent based on the median composite ACT score.

[4] Cost of attendance includes tuition, fees, room and board, and other necessary expenses. Statistics reported for two-year institutions reflect costs excluding room and board since they are restricted to nonresidential institutions in this analysis.

COA and then discounting it with either need-based or merit-based financial aid for all or most students is a form of marketing.

Table 1.5 reports statistics regarding institutional finances. One clear conclusion that emerges from this table is that it is difficult for other institutions to compete with those private institutions that have large endowments. The median institution in this group has an endowment per student of $341,900. At a typical spending rate of 4.5 percent, their endowments generate a median draw over $15,000 per student per year. Those institutions also receive tuition revenue about twice as high as other privates and public flagships/R1 institutions (this does not include room and board, which is not included as a "core revenue" or "core expenditure" in IPEDS data). It is no surprise, based on these data, that they are able to spend considerably more per student, as shown in the bottom panel of the table. In fact, institutions with the highest endowment values spend considerably more per student than the full COA that they charge to students who receive no financial aid (not shown).

Note that the median investment return for private institutions with large endowments was very high in 2018 (over $28,000 per student), contributing to stated revenues per student well in excess of expenditures. That amount reflects investment success in the endowments' portfolios; 2018 was a year with high investment returns. These institutions do not spend those returns immediately, though. They contribute to the endowment, and money is withdrawn from that pool at some predetermined rate (like the 4.5 percent approximation used earlier).

Revenues and expenditures at public flagship and R1 institutions follow behind those values at private institutions with large endowments. They collect more in tuition and fees, greater financial support from the state, and more grant funding than other public four-year institutions. They use those greater resources to spend more money on instruction and research.

Another notable conclusion from this table is the similarity in the finances of a private four-year institution with a smaller endowment and a public four-year institution that is neither a flagship nor R1. Both types of institutions spend about the same amount per student and receive similar amounts of revenue. They both spend the same amount of money on instruction and little on research. Their administrative expenses are allocated differently, but that may represent accounting differences more than substantive differences. The private institutions receive more revenue in the form of tuition, and the public institutions receive funding from the state, but they balance.

TABLE 1.5 Institution financial profiles for fiscal 2018, by type of institution[1]

	4-Year Institutions				Public 2-Year
	Public Flagship/ R1	Other Public	High-Endowment Private	Other Private	
	Endowments and Endowment Spending				
Endowment per FTE	$26,000	$6,200	$341,900	$26,100	$1,300
Endow. Spending per FTE (Assumed to be 4.5 percent)	$1,200	$300	$15,400	$1,200	$100
	Revenues per FTE				
Tuition and Fees[2]	$12,100	$6,700	$26,400	$15,100	$2,400
State and Local Governments	$8,000	$6,200	$0	$0	$6,600
Investment Returns	$700	$100	$28,100	$1,800	$0
Government Grants/Contracts[2]	$7,600	$3,600	$1,200	$400	$3,900
Private Gifts/ Grants/Contracts	$3,100	$500	$13,800	$2,800	$100
Other Core Revenues	$4,400	$1,800	$2,300	$600	$700
Total Core Revenue[3]	$35,900	$18,900	$71,800	$20,700	$13,700
Total Revenue	$45,900	$25,100	$91,900	$29,800	$17,700
	Expenditures per FTE				
Instruction	$13,100	$8,500	$23,600	$9,100	$5,900
Research	$8,000	$300	$1,100	$0	$0
Institutional Support	$3,100	$2,700	$11,100	$5,100	$2,200
Student Services	$1,800	$2,200	$8,600	$4,500	$1,600
Academic Support	$3,600	$2,200	$6,700	$2,000	$1,200
Public Service	$2,700	$500	$100	$0	$0
Other	$2,400	$2,400	$0	$0	$2,200
Total Core Expenditures[3]	$34,700	$18,800	$51,200	$20,700	$13,100
Total Expenditures	$44,600	$24,800	$67,000	$27,900	$17,000

Source: Author's calculations based on data from IPEDS.

Note: FTE represents full-time-equivalent student.

[1] All statistics represent median values within categories. All categories except for public two-year institutions are restricted to institutions where dorm capacity is at least 25 percent of the undergraduate population (i.e., "residential"). Two-year institutions are restricted to nonresidential.

[2] Different accounting standards between public and private universities complicated comparisons across types of institutions. For instance, Pell Grants are included in tuition and fees at private institutions, but they are included as grants at public institutions.

[3] Does not include expenses/revenue from auxiliary services, including room and board.

The finances of two-year public institutions are considerably different than any of the other types of institutions. The vast majority of their funding comes from the government in the form of direct subsidies and Pell Grants. Limited tuition and fees are collected, reflecting the income status of their students; 55 percent receive Pell Grants. They receive considerably less revenue and spend less than the other types of institutions.

Overall, tables 1.4 and 1.5 demonstrate that two-year institutions are considerably different than any of the categories of four-year institutions. They have fewer resources, serve more students from lower-income families, enroll students with varying academic preparation (as measured by test scores, although test scores are typically not required at these institutions), and have very low graduation rates. This is a critical sector of the higher-education market in terms of the population served, but the issues these institutions face are very different than those that residential four-year colleges and universities face. That sector deserves separate attention that is beyond the scope of this book.

For the remaining types of institutions considered, these data demonstrate that they all have distinct characteristics in terms of their revenue streams, how they spend their money, and their financial aid systems. The remainder of this book will continue to segment the higher-education market using these categories.

CHAPTER TWO

An Econ 101 View of College Pricing and Financial Aid

The preceding chapter addressed the details of how the financial aid system operates in the real world, highlighting much of its complexity. But complexity has a way of hindering understanding. One concept that students in an introductory economics course learn is the value of abstraction. Because the world is a complicated place, we must make simplifying assumptions, setting aside the nuanced and less essential real-world features that can obscure our understanding of how markets work. Economics leverages abstraction in its analytical framework.

The purpose of this chapter is to introduce this analytical framework to describe college pricing and financial aid using basic economic concepts. The higher-education market has consumers (students) and firms (colleges and universities) who meet in a marketplace where prices, inclusive of financial aid, are determined. I address three standard questions that economists often ask about the functioning of individual markets: (1) How are prices set in this market? (2) Are there market "imperfections"—things like limited information or market power—that prevent the pricing system from functioning well? (3) Are there ways the government can intervene to help?

The bulk of the chapter represents material similar to that which I present to the Econ 101: Introduction to Microeconomics class that I routinely teach. In fact, some of this discussion is taken from the lectures I deliver in that class. At the end of the chapter, I summarize this material and discuss the lessons learned. Since there is no final exam in this course, readers are not penalized for skipping right to that discussion if they prefer.

Throughout the discussion, I will continue to concentrate on four-year residential public and private colleges and universities. I will also focus on pricing and financial aid for domestic students and, at public institutions, state residents. International students and out-of-state students are important sources of revenue for higher-educational institutions but incorporating strategic decisions regarding them will distract from my main focus on financial aid. I also ignore issues associated with targeted scholarships like those for athletes. These are examples of abstraction.

How Are Prices Set?

A Stylized Description of the College Pricing System

The simplest way to characterize college pricing is to describe the relationship between a family's ability to pay, as captured by the expected family contribution (EFC), and what they actually pay after factoring in financial aid, or the net price. Figure 2.1 does so, distinguishing institutions that meet full need (the dotted line) from those that do not (the solid lines). The peak price at meet-full-need institutions is higher than the peak price at institutions that do not meet full need, which is consistent with the data reported in chapter 1 (the majority of schools in the large-endowment, private institution category in table 1.4 meet full need). This figure also incorporates

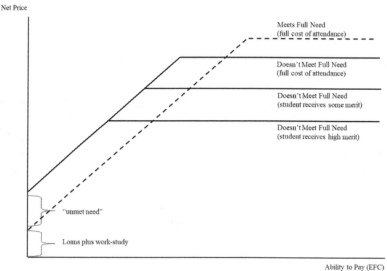

FIGURE 2.1. College pricing by type of financial aid system

merit awards as an option for schools that do not meet full need. Recall that "financial aid" includes both need-based awards and merit-based awards. Some schools that meet full need do also offer merit awards, but they do so to a much smaller number of students; I ignore that possibility here.

In the figure, students who cannot afford to pay anything at a meets-full-need institution still pay a positive net price—it represents federal loans and work-study funding that the institution may expect from a student (I ignore minimum student contributions in this discussion). These institutions do not expect any payments beyond that. A need-based financial aid award will cover the entire difference between that net price and the cost of attendance (COA). As family financial resources rise, the net price increases dollar for dollar with the greater ability to pay (higher EFC); the slope of the dotted line is one. This pattern continues until ability to pay rises to the level of the full COA at those institutions. At that point, the student is projected to be able to afford that cost, and no financial aid is offered. For families with even greater financial resources, the cost remains constant at the full COA.

The key distinction between schools that meet full need and those that do not is the presence of unmet need. This is represented in figure 2.1 as a gap between the dotted and solid lines; this is related to the concept of gapping, described in chapter 1. Students at these institutions are expected to pay an additional amount beyond what is calculated as affordable for them. They would be expected to find that funding elsewhere (like additional loans, greater earnings, outside scholarships, or gifts from relatives).

That gap remains as ability to pay rises. The size of that gap is determined by the college's specific financial aid policy; the two lines do not need to be parallel. In other words, there is no reason for institutions that do not meet full need to charge an additional dollar for every additional dollar a student's family can afford to pay. The slope of this line may be less than one. Regardless, for students who do not receive merit awards, the net price is capped by the full COA, which may be triggered at a lower ability to pay than at a school that meets full need, as shown in the figure. This is partly attributable to the lower sticker price that these institutions tend to charge, but it also occurs because they do not meet full need.

For students who receive merit awards from the institution, the amount of those awards contributes to their ability to pay. That lessens their financial need and reduces the level of need-based financial aid they will receive. In the diagram, for simplicity I show that a student otherwise eligible for need-based aid (on the sloped portion of the net price line) who receives a merit award loses that need-based aid dollar for dollar, leaving the net price unchanged. Receipt of a merit award from the institution may not fully off-set need-based aid, but at least a large share of it will. Students with no financial need—those who can afford to pay the full sticker price—receive a discount in their net price of the full amount of the award. They are the students who truly benefit from a merit award.

Market Power and the Economics of "Price Discrimination"

As a college professor, my job is to teach economics to the students in my classes. They attend my lectures, come see me during office hours, complete problem sets, and take exams. Students differ in the effort they put into their education, but they all have access to the same educational services that my colleagues and I provide to them.

If I teach a class of thirty students, though, statistics suggest that perhaps ten to fifteen of them paid the full COA. (Wellesley College is a private institution with a large endowment that meets full need. Around 60 percent of students receive need-based financial aid; it offers no merit aid.) The others paid less than that, some of them considerably less. For the most part, I have no idea which students are paying how much. They all receive the same educational services.

Setting a range of prices for different customers purchasing the same good is not the way that prices are determined in a typical competitive market. In competitive markets, prices are determined by the interaction of supply and demand (if students learn nothing else from my class, they need to learn that!); everyone pays the single price set by the market. If one firm tried to set a price higher than anyone else, no one would buy from that firm. If someone could purchase the good at a lower price, they would do so and resell it at a profit at the market price. The price is the price, and everyone pays the same thing.

Another commonly covered topic in a typical Econ 101 class is the issue of market power. A firm has market power when it has the ability to directly influence the price—it does not just come from the interaction of supply and demand in the broader market. This happens when there are a small number of firms that dominate the market.

For example, think of the airlines. As of this writing, only two airlines fly between Boston and Dallas (JetBlue and American). This is not a competitive market; the airlines have some market power over the cost of these flights. That is very different from the case of, say, the local supermarket in a city or suburb that is limited in terms of how much they can charge for a gallon of milk, because there are plenty of other options for consumers to buy milk. Milk at one supermarket is perfectly substitutable for milk at another supermarket.

One thing a firm with market power can do to maximize its profit is engage in what economists call "price discrimination." This so-called discrimination is not illegal and it is not based on someone's race, gender, or nationality. Rather, it is based on a perceived willingness or ability to pay. Standard examples include airline pricing for business versus leisure travelers (business travelers are willing to pay more) and different movie ticket prices for senior citizens (typically, senior citizens are not willing to pay as much as younger individuals).

College pricing is another common example of price discrimination (see Mankiw, 2021). Perfect price discrimination is an extreme form of that concept where each consumer pays a different price specific to them. This is frequently what happens in the market for a college education.

The typical textbook coverage of price discrimination indicates that it can only occur if the market has three characteristics: (1) firms have market power, (2) firms can distinguish across consumers by willingness to pay, and (3) no resale of the product is possible. Again, firms have market power when there are fewer of them and they have some control over price. When there are a lot of firms competing, traditional rules of supply and demand hold and the price is determined by the market, not firms. Price discrimination is only possible for firms with market power. The second condition, that firms need to be able to distinguish consumers by willingness to pay, is required so that firms can figure out how much to charge to whom. Those willing to pay more will be charged more. Finally, if the product can be resold, then those consumers charged a lower price could buy a lot of the product and resell it, undercutting the firm.

The educational services that colleges and universities provide satisfy these conditions. They derive market power from the fact that institutions have distinctive characteristics or at least are clustered into smaller groups that have similarly distinctive characteristics (liberal arts versus research university, urban versus rural, STEM versus arts focus, *US News* rankings, etc.). Of course, similar institutions compete, but the extent of competition is diminished. Since the higher-education market is made up of many institutions that are not perfectly substitutable, they have market power.

Higher-educational institutions are able to distinguish their customers' willingness to pay different prices by requiring students seeking aid to complete comprehensive financial aid forms. In fact, the entire purpose of the financial aid application process, from the perspective of higher-educational institutions, is to determine ability to pay (recall the concept of EFC, from chapter 1). The detailed financial information provided in those applications enables institutions to perfectly price discriminate.

Note that students' willingness to pay is not entirely determined by ability to pay, but they certainly are related. Two wealthy students may place different weights on the value of an education at particular institutions, but those students almost certainly are willing to pay more than students from lower-income families, who have a limited ability to pay for college even if they value it highly.

The third condition necessary for price discrimination is that individuals cannot resell the product they purchased. Clearly a college education satisfies this condition.

In the end, all three requirements for price discrimination are met. The extent of individualized information on ability to pay allows institutions to perfectly price discriminate (up to the value of the sticker price). Students with greater family financial resources pay more, and families with fewer family financial resources pay less.

Pricing at Different Types of Institutions

Market power plays a significant role in the extent to which firms can price discriminate. In a competitive market, firms cannot price discriminate at all because all products are assumed to be the same and easily substitutable. A monopoly (only one firm in the industry) has the greatest market power because there are no substitutes available. A gradient in market power exists between these two extremes. The easier it is to find an alternative supplier and the closer the substitute products available, the less market power. Firms with less market power cannot differentiate prices as much as firms with more market power. Consumers are not willing to pay a lot more for a particular product if there are readily available substitutes.

This matters in higher education because different types of institutions have different amounts of market power (Epple et al., 2019). Consider the market for the most elite institutions. Harvard, Princeton, Stanford, Yale, and perhaps a few others compete in a market of their own. Among those students with sufficient resources, willingness to pay is high, enabling these institutions to charge a high sticker price. Many elite public institutions (the University of Michigan, the University of Virginia and some others) have similar market power, although there are limits placed on their ability to use it, a topic that is discussed below.

Among less prestigious institutions, there are dozens of schools competing for the same students. These institutions have less market power. They work hard to distinguish themselves from each other (academic program, geography, and the like), but it is harder with such a large number. One could imagine they still have some control over the price—some students may be willing to pay more to attend their favorite institution relative to others—but certainly less than at more elite schools. This market is more competitive, albeit not perfectly competitive. Recall that "competitive" in the context of this book does not address the difficulty of getting accepted at an institution, but the extent of market power held by schools. Harvard is more competitive in the admissions sense, but it holds more market power and is less competitive in that sense.

In terms of pricing, these less prestigious institutions with less market power can still discriminate on the basis of price, but not quite as much. The difference between willingness to pay and ability to pay becomes more important. Although the two are clearly linked, they do not need to be identical. Wealthier students may be able to afford to pay a large amount to attend a specific institution. Why would they, though, if they could attend any one of the multitude of competitors and pay less? They may still be willing to pay somewhat more to attend their favorite institution, but not a lot more.

The Impact of a Price Ceiling at Public Institutions

At public institutions, the relatively low caps on COA set by states for its residents represent a form of price ceiling. The standard example of a price ceiling in an Econ 101 course is rent control (Mankiw, 2021). Consider a perfectly competitive market for rental housing where the rental price is determined by supply and demand. The market price is considered to be too high, so a law is passed imposing a ceiling prohibiting rents above some level to be charged.

Economic analysis indicates that those policies will result in a shortage of rental housing, among other problems. The shortage enables landlords to be selective in terms of who rents the apartment. One possible response is to favor higher-income tenants who are more likely to make their monthly payments, violating the policy's intention of providing affordable housing to lower-income tenants.

In the market for higher education, price ceilings have a similar unintended consequence, although the mechanism is different. Here, when a state sets a relatively low sticker price, it is essentially imposing a price ceiling. Prices cannot rise above that level. The fact that sticker prices at public institutions are considerably lower than those at private institutions suggests that these price ceilings are binding. Prices at these institutions are capped at levels lower than they likely would be otherwise.

In the presence of a market that is characterized by perfect price discrimination, this price ceiling reduces the price paid by students from higher-income families. They are the ones who would have paid a net price that is more than the state-mandated sticker price otherwise. This price ceiling lowers revenue from these otherwise high-paying students, reducing funding that could be made available for financial aid. In the end, students from higher-income families are helped and students from lower-income families may be hurt by a policy whose intention is to make college more affordable.

Spillovers from the Public to the Private Sector

Competition in the market extends the impact of a low sticker price policy at public institutions to the private institutions that compete with them. For the most part, private institutions with large endowments do not compete directly with public institutions. This is clear based on the much higher sticker price that these institutions charge relative to public institutions, which I documented in chapter 1.

But other private institutions do compete more directly with public institutions. They would have difficulty recruiting higher-income students if they charged a lot more than public institutions. This shows up in their sticker prices, which are between those of public institutions and private institutions with large endowments.

But the sticker price that these private institutions charge is misleading because of the extent to which they offer merit awards. As I showed in table 1.4, the median private institution with a smaller endowment provides financial aid to virtually all its students. For those students with higher incomes, this aid is provided in the form of merit, as represented in figure 2.1. Such an institution has a stated COA, but few students end up paying that much. Effectively, the maximum price is set at the COA less the minimum merit award that the institution provides.

This pricing strategy further reduces the differential between the COA at these private institutions and public institutions. Again, this demonstrates the extent of competition between these two segments of the market. In reducing the effective COA at private institutions, competition also lowers the resources available to be used for financial aid for lower-income students at those institutions.

Why do these private institutions use this pricing strategy? Why do they not just set the COA at the effective maximum price instead of attaching merit aid to a higher COA? One potential (likely?) answer is its role in marketing. A higher stated COA may send a signal of higher quality. Providing merit to reduce the amount paid also provides a feeling of accomplishment to the student. Students like to feel that they are meritorious and wanted by the institution. This form of marketing behavior is no different than a manufacturer placing a high sticker price on its product knowing that the retailer will mark the price down immediately.

Are Market Imperfections Costly in Higher Education?

Standard economic analysis indicates that perfectly competitive markets have many beneficial properties: efficient production and low prices that deliver the greatest possible benefit to society. Markets that deviate from perfect competition (which are labeled "imperfectly competitive") take away from that. When firms have market power, it reduces those benefits, resulting in market inefficiencies. When firms cooperate with each other, known as collusion, it is also harmful. Efficiency is only maintained with perfect information on the part of all parties involved in the market, especially consumers.

How do these concepts of imperfect competition and the damage they generate in more traditional markets translate to the market for higher education? The impact may not be the same because higher education is not a standard market. Its nonprofit nature (at least the portion of the market that I address) is one important difference; I describe its relevance below.

The concept of equity also takes on a far more prominent role in our evaluation of the higher-education market than in other industries. In economics, we generally recognize that market outcomes may not be "fair." They do not treat the rich and the poor the same, and we often accept that inequity (although we do implement programs to undo extreme disadvantage through social welfare policies). Those who are rich tend to drive nice cars that the poor cannot afford, and we ordinarily accept that.

With a college education, though, the inequity also results in market inefficiencies. A college education is an investment. If the college pricing system prevents lower-income students from making otherwise worthwhile investments, that is inefficient. Students could borrow to make the investment, but difficulty obtaining sufficient credit or aversion to the risk associated with that much debt may prevent them from doing so.

The bottom line is that creating economic opportunity through affordable college pricing is good for society. Standard forms of market imperfections that usually are costly to society, like market power and collusion, may actually be beneficial in this market. Perfect information, though, remains necessary for the market to function properly. The next section provides further detail to justify these conclusions.

The Role of Market Power

As I discussed earlier, it is the existence of market power that enables higher-educational institutions to perfectly price discriminate. In a traditional market, firms that engage in that behavior harm consumers by charging each of them the maximum price they are willing to pay and help themselves by earning excessive profits.

The colleges and universities that are the focus of my analysis, though, are nonprofit institutions. In that market, the fact that colleges and universities have market power and perfectly price discriminate offers some advantages. Students with greater family financial resources who are willing and able to pay more are charged more, generating additional funds for the institution. Those funds can be used to enroll students with limited financial resources who are willing and able to pay less. The institution will incur a loss on those students. This system works as long as the surplus from the more affluent students is sufficient to cover the losses from the less affluent. This would not happen if these institutions were organized as for-profit entities because the surplus is profit for them. It would not be used to benefit others.

One implication of this system is that it generates the paradox that higher sticker prices may actually improve educational opportunities for lower-income students. When sticker prices rise, students from wealthy families pay more. That additional revenue can be used to enroll more students from lower-income families who can afford to pay less.

This model of perfect price discrimination provides implications that may be unsatisfying to students from higher-income families. For them, a literal interpretation of this model is that colleges and universities are profiting off them and then taking the money to subsidize others.

This implication, though, ignores other sources of revenues that institutions receive, particularly those institutions that meet full need, which are typically private institutions with large endowments. At those institutions, endowment support flows to all students. In chapter 1, I showed that the median private four-year institution with a large endowment generates around $15,000 per student per year in spending from its endowment. The endowments at these schools provide regular revenue that supplements the operating income earned from student payments. Indeed, the $71,000 sticker price at those institutions, shown in table 1.4, is similar to total spending per student of $67,000, shown in table 1.5 (the very highly endowed institutions, not separately reported here, spend considerably more per student than the revenue they receive from students). Institutions mainly do not profit from higher-income students; they just lose less from educating them.

One can think of this system as one where higher-income students largely pay their own way and other sources of revenue, including endowment spending, are used to subsidize the cost of lower-income students. State funding may be thought of similarly at public institutions. Either way, this system creates a way to provide access to higher education for students who otherwise would have difficulty paying for it.

Collusion and the Prisoner's Dilemma

Collusion among firms is definitely considered to be harmful in standard economic models. If two firms collude, they simulate the market outcome that would occur if there were just a single firm—a monopoly. The greater market power held by the firms acting as a monopoly would force consumers to pay more, thereby transferring more resources from consumers to the firms and creating additional "deadweight loss" (resources that are lost to society). It is routinely frowned upon.

In the context of financial aid, though, there are instances when collusion may be beneficial. Merit aid is one such instance. Many institutions offer merit aid, which is awarded in greater value to students with stronger academic records. Clearly, institutions offer these awards to enroll these students who might otherwise choose to enroll elsewhere.

The problem is that if all institutions offer this form of merit aid, it does not change the market outcome and limits their revenue. This is a phenomenon called the "prisoner's dilemma," which McPherson and Schapiro

(1998) address extensively in the context of higher education. In its classic context, the prisoner's dilemma exists when two crime suspects are arrested and the police seek confessions from both to seal a conviction with a stiff penalty. As any viewer of television police shows knows, the first thing the police do after arresting the two suspects is to place them in separate interrogation rooms. Then the investigator in each room tells each suspect that the other is seeking a plea deal that would implicate him or her. Not wanting to be on the wrong side of that deal, they confess and implicate the other suspect. Both suspects succumb to the ploy and dual confessions are obtained.

The critical aspect of the prisoner's dilemma is that both suspects likely would have received more lenient treatment if they both remained silent. The incentives, though, are inconsistent with that approach because neither suspect trusts that the other will abide by a promised vow of silence. The solution to their problem is some form of contract that binds them both to keep that promise. Without some form of binding constraint, the agreement will be broken by both parties.

Colleges offering merit awards face similar issues. If two colleges are competing for students, the best outcome for both institutions would be to avoid offering merit aid and collect the students' full willingness to pay—perhaps the full COA. The problem is that both institutions have an incentive to "cheat" on that arrangement. If one offers merit awards, it is likely to get more or better students. The other views the problem the same way. In the end, they both offer the merit award and attract the same students at a lower price. Both institutions would have been better off avoiding the offer of merit funding. This is a prisoner's dilemma.

Since merit awards typically displace at least a large share of need-based awards, the students who benefit from their existence are those who can afford to pay more. In the prisoner's dilemma, students end up choosing the same school they would have chosen if no schools offered merit aid, but higher-educational institutions receive less revenue from higher-income students. Again, this is money that could have been used to offer more need-based aid to lower-income students.

The Role of Imperfect Information

A fundamental conclusion from the discussion earlier in this chapter is that perfect price discrimination has the ability to improve college access. It provides institutions with the resources necessary to reduce the price for lower-income students below their cost, potentially enabling them to enroll in college.

Of course, that cannot happen if nobody knows what those prices are. A system that charges students from higher-income families considerably more than students from lower-income families will not work if the only price anyone knows is the price paid by students from higher-income families. This does not promote college access. It convinces lower-income students that they cannot afford college when it is possible that they can. It is difficult to justify the existence of imperfect information in the market. To the extent that it exists, it must be resolved for the system to be effective. Doing so will be one of the themes in the remainder of this book.

The Role of Government in the Market for Higher Education

The government intervenes in the higher-education market in several ways that are designed to promote affordability in college pricing. These include efforts to enhance competition through antitrust policy, price setting at public colleges and universities, and directly providing need-based financial aid. We can use economic analysis to evaluate the ability of these interventions to accomplish their goal. This section provides that analysis.

Antitrust Policy

Market power typically harms the social good, increasing prices consumers pay, transferring resources from consumers to producers, and generating "deadweight loss" (again, resources that are lost to society). A common response to this problem is to implement antitrust policy designed to increase the level of competition in the marketplace to take advantage of the benefits that such competition typically offers.

But charging higher prices to students from higher-income families helps support a financial aid system that charges lower prices to students from lower-income families. The question is whether society is better off by imposing these higher prices on higher-income students. I believe one could credibly argue that the answer to this question is yes. If so, then antitrust policy is harmful, not helpful.

Consider, for instance, the efforts of the US Department of Justice in 1991, which sought to increase competition in the higher-educational marketplace by preventing a select group of elite private institutions from coordinating the financial aid awards they offered to students. To end the investigation, the institutions agreed to stop the practice (Reed and Shireman, 2008). Perhaps the meetings of school representatives discussing individual students' finances were unwarranted, but the cooperation among the institutions to maintain affordability for all students had value. Salop and White (1991) provide an extensive discussion of this antitrust dispute, concluding that "the colleges' strongest point might be that society's overall educational and social goals are better served by limiting the amount of financial aid to the most desired students to permit more poor students overall to attend college, given the competing demands on college budgets" (200). This is consistent with the views I am presenting here.

More recently, the US Department of Justice similarly intervened in the market, attempting to increase competition and lower prices, with a similar impact. The issue was the National Association of College Admission Counseling (NACAC) policy against "poaching" (Jaschik, 2019). This policy was an agreement among higher-educational institutions not to (among other things):

1. offer incentives, including greater financial aid, to students to submit early decision applications;
2. recruit and offer incentives to accepted students who have already submitted a deposit at another institution;
3. recruit and offer incentives to enrolled students at other institutions to transfer.

Rather than continue what would likely have been a protracted and expensive legal battle with the Department of Justice, NACAC backed down and agreed to eliminate these provisions at their 2019 annual meeting.

The agreement had represented a legitimate solution to the prisoner's dilemma problem. The dilemma is that institutions competing over students have an incentive to poach. That incentive is greater for higher-paying students, who generate more revenue for the institution. If both institutions make such offers to the same student, the enrollment outcome will be the same, but the revenue collected from the student will fall. If the institutions cooperated, agreeing not to undertake that sort of activity, the prisoner's dilemma would be avoided. NACAC's policy change under Justice Department pressure to end this practice restores the prisoner's dilemma. The revenue collected from higher-income students will fall, leaving fewer resources available to the institutions to charge less to lower-income students.

Cooperative agreements reducing the use of merit awards would also be a beneficial policy that would run afoul of traditional antitrust policies. It should be encouraged nonetheless. I addressed this issue earlier as an example of the prisoner's dilemma problem in which institutions offer merit to entice students. The plan backfires, though, because all institutions have this incentive, making similar offers of merit.

In the end, all students end up attending the same school they would have attended otherwise, but institutional revenue is diminished. Students from wealthier families are the main beneficiaries from these awards because the offer of merit to a student from a lower-income family displaces need-based aid. It also reduces revenues that could have otherwise been used to provide greater need-based financial aid. In this case as well, antitrust policy is not beneficial to society.

The Role of Price Setting at Public Institutions

At public institutions, the COA is set by the states either through a separate state agency or by the legislature itself (see Zinth and Smith, 2012, and Education Commission of the States, 2020, for details). A critical component of the political process in setting that amount is the concept of affordability. Politicians are loath to set prices that would be perceived as unaffordable by their constituency. They face significant pressure to keep prices "low" (or not so high since few people view them as low).

Maintaining a lower maximum price, though, reduces college affordability for lower-income students attending those public institutions as well as for those attending private institutions with whom those public institutions compete. As I highlighted earlier, lower sticker prices reduce the revenue from higher-income students and constrain an institution's ability to provide greater financial aid to lower-income students. Private institutions that compete with these public entities have no choice but to stay at least within the range of what these public institutions charge. This prevents them from collecting the necessary revenue to subsidize college costs of lower-income families.

Why do states set their sticker prices at their current levels? One perspective is based on a misunderstanding of the economics of college costs and financial aid. A low sticker price is considered desirable because it makes college affordable, the thinking goes. How else is a student from a family making, say, $30,000 or even $50,000 per year supposed to afford college if we set the sticker price too high?

Of course, they cannot. That is the point of the financial aid system: to reduce the cost for this family so that their children can attend college. Yet keeping the sticker price low actually makes it harder for the financial aid system to accomplish that goal. It is possible that the complexities inherent in the system lead to a misunderstanding of this issue among policy makers.

Alternatively, the current system may result from the politics of college tuition setting. It is well known that the pool of voters skews considerably toward higher-income households. According to Akee (2019), 80 percent of families with incomes between $100,000 and $150,000 vote in elections, compared to around 55 percent of those with incomes between $20,000 and $30,000. Keeping the COA more affordable for this higher-income group may be politically advantageous. Of course, accomplishing that goal makes it more difficult to maintain affordability for lower-income families. Either way, the political process that results in lower sticker prices is harmful to college access for lower-income students.

Public Goods and Free College

Economists generally frown on intervening directly in markets unless there is a very good reason. In some cases, the nature of the good prevents a market system from achieving the best outcome for society. In these instances, government intervention is warranted.

One example is when the product is a "public good." Public goods have two defining characteristics; they are said to be "nonrival" and "nonexcludable." A good is nonrival if one person's enjoyment of it does not affect another's enjoyment of exactly the same item. If I buy an ice cream cone, I would be very upset if a stranger tried to consume it too (especially if it were Ben and Jerry's Chunky Monkey!). That characterizes a rival good. A nonrival good is one that is easy to "share." If I am watching *The Irishman* on Netflix, I do not care if someone else is watching it at the same time. That is nonrival.

A good is said to be nonexcludable if it is difficult to prevent someone from consuming a product once it is produced. If I buy an ice cream cone, I do not have to share it with you. Hulu can prevent you from watching *Nomadland* because you cannot watch it without a subscription. These are excludable goods. Fish in a local pond, however, are nonexcludable. Anyone can fish in the pond and hope to land the big one (as long as there is no overfishing). They are rival, though, because if I catch one, I would prefer to eat it myself without sharing.

For a good to be a public good, it must be nonrival and nonexcludable. Public parks and national defense are common examples. We all consume them simultaneously (ignoring crowding issues in the park), and we cannot exclude anyone from receiving the benefits.

If there is demand for a public good, the government should provide it. Individuals will be averse to use their own funds to purchase something that they can use for free if others pay for it to be produced. This is called the "free rider" problem. For society to receive the benefits of this good, the government should produce it because private producers have insufficient incentive to provide it. Again, public parks and national defense illustrate the point.

In terms of higher education, it is common to hear claims that the government should provide it because it is a public good (see Kim, 2019, and Warner, 2019, as examples). This argument has been used recently to support the policy proposal of free college, endorsed by 2020 presidential candidates Bernie Sanders and Elizabeth Warren, among others. If higher education satisfied the definition of a public good, free college would be justified.

Yet higher education does not satisfy the necessary conditions (Preston, 2017, makes this point as well). One could make a case that it is nonrival, at least to some extent. If another student is added to a class, it is unlikely to have a substantial impact on the education received by other students. Of course, crowding would be an issue, but that would be true with a public park as well. Higher education is excludable, though. The entire purpose of the admissions process is to admit some students and exclude others. And if you do not pay your tuition, you cannot attend classes. In essence, it is no different than Hulu. Public provision on that basis does not make sense.

Higher Education and Positive Externalities

This does not mean that there is no role for the government to intervene in the higher-education marketplace. A better argument for doing so is based on the concept of a positive externality. A positive externality is a benefit to society that a good generates that goes beyond the benefits received by those participating in the transaction. When I buy an ice cream cone, it makes me happy and it generates revenue for the ice cream shop, but it has no impact on others, so there is no externality. When I buy flowers to plant in my yard, it makes me happy and it makes all of my neighbors happy. When I get vaccinated against a disease, I am protected, but so are others with whom I come into contact. In these cases, others receive a benefit that they did not have to pay for based on my actions. That is a positive externality.

Colleges provide positive externalities in many ways. In simple ways, having a college in your community is a lot like the flowers—it is nice having a quiet, landscaped area in your community. Some may say, though, that campuses may generate negative externalities as well—crowded streets, difficult parking, unruly students, and the like.

But those very localized effects pale in comparison to the positive externalities that higher-educational institutions bring to society more broadly. For instance, college graduates are more likely to be civic leaders. From an economic standpoint, colleges train individuals who will become business leaders, entrepreneurs, scientists, and members of a more highly skilled workforce. That generates more economic activity, which benefits everyone. For instance, Moretti (2004) finds evidence that having a larger share of college graduates in a community, which brings increased spending from their earnings advantage, leads to higher wages among those who dropped out of high school and those with only a high school degree.

Yet standard economic models indicate that markets will not produce enough goods that generate positive externalities without government intervention. The standard solution to this problem is to subsidize consumption. In the case of higher education, that would mean reducing the cost of attending college for students, providing them with an incentive to attend.

This solution, though, relies on the notion that all consumers pay the same price. If so, then the correct policy response is to provide an equal subsidy to all students to encourage attendance.

But not all students need to be subsidized to encourage them to attend. Many students would attend college even without the subsidy. They are already willing to pay at least as much as the COA. We do not need to subsidize them to get them to enroll. They will do so anyway.

The students who will respond to the subsidy are those whose ability to pay may be lower, and that is linked to students from lower-income families. They cannot afford the market price. For them, providing a subsidy may encourage enrollment.

Normally, the ability to target subsidies to groups that are more likely to respond to them is difficult, but the financial aid system in higher education facilitates that. The same information used to price discriminate (i.e., calculation of ability to pay) can be used to target these subsidies. They could come in the form of federally provided financial aid that is income contingent. This justifies a program like Pell Grants.

So why does the government provide free K-12 education to all children? The reason is because a K-12 education generates very large public returns, and a college education leads to very large private returns. It would be difficult to function as a society without children receiving a baseline level of education that enables them to read and write and to perform basic mathematical operations (the three Rs). We need all children to master those basic skills in a democracy with a modern economy. Obtaining any form of employment and avoiding criminal activity, extensive drug use, or other forms of costly social behavior is easier with a primary education. College, on the other hand, provides large private benefits in the form of higher lifetime earnings to students who attend (a lengthier discussion of this point is provided in chapter 3). With such a large private return, subsidizing a college education for all students, many of whom would choose to attend anyway, is unnecessary.

Summary and Discussion

The purpose of this chapter is to provide a broad, analytical framework for how pricing works in the higher-education marketplace in practice and how it could work better in order to provide greater access to students from lower-income households. The main conceptual point that runs throughout the chapter is the notion of perfect price discrimination. The requirement that students complete the FAFSA and perhaps the CSS Profile provides institutions with precise information about a family's finances, which is used to determine how much they can afford to pay. The ability to charge different prices to each student facilitates access because lower-income students can be charged less.

The question is whether there is enough money in the system to price discriminate enough so that students from lower-income families can actually afford to attend. Typically, private institutions that have large endowments have enough of a niche in the marketplace that they have considerable control over their own prices. They can price discriminate to a greater extent, charging higher-income students more, potentially a lot more, than lower-income students. This additional revenue helps cover the costs of admitting lower-income students and charging them an amount at, or at least close to, what they can afford. Spending from their endowments also enables them to accomplish this.

This system breaks down somewhat outside of that small, elite sector of the higher-education market. Greater competition between the much larger number of institutions in the rest of the market complicate the ability to perfectly price discriminate. If these institutions charge significantly higher prices to students from higher-income families, they can be undercut in the market by one of the many similar institutions with which they compete. Public institutions are further constrained by a COA that is capped by state policy makers in an attempt to maintain affordability, even though that cap is binding only on higher-income students.

The lower sticker prices at public institutions make it even harder for the less well-endowed private institutions to charge a high sticker price. Merit awards that are available to a large share (all?) of an institutions' students are one response. These awards are used to enable the private institutions to charge a higher sticker price, potentially in an attempt to signal quality, and then reduce the maximum amount students actually have to pay. These institutions face restrictions on revenue from higher-income students that limit the amount that could be used to support need-based financial aid.

Additional merit awards that are offered to students with strong qualifications contribute to this problem as well. These awards may reflect a prisoner's dilemma, which generates an important inefficiency. Schools provide discounts trying to attract "better" students that, in the end, do not change anyone's behavior, since all of the competing schools do the same thing. Resources are devoted to the chase, without impact, which could have been used to support more need-based financial aid.

Without significant outside resources and without the ability to charge enough of a premium to higher-income students, these institutions simply do not have the funding to enroll lower-income students at prices they can afford. These institutions ask for payments from these students that are beyond the students' means because they need to pay their bills.

In terms of public policy, this may be a rare exception where promoting competition may not improve the public good. Antitrust policies promoted over the past few decades in the higher-education arena have contributed to the problem. Increased competition makes it harder for colleges and universities to price discriminate, and that reduces access to college for students from lower-income families.

Standard economic reasoning, however, does provide justification for direct subsidies to promote college enrollment via the positive externalities it generates. Indeed, financial aid applications, which enable the government and institutions to determine a student's ability to pay, can help with this. They enable those subsidies to be narrowly targeted to students from lower-income families, who may need them to enroll. Higher-income students already have the resources necessary to cover the cost, and they still receive the significant private returns that a college education can provide. It is still a good investment for them.

Subsidizing the cost of college for lower-income students not only improves the efficiency of the higher-education marketplace, but it is also a more equitable solution as well. A fundamental problem in economics is the common trade-off between equity and efficiency. Public policies designed to accomplish one goal often fail to satisfy the other. This is a rare example of a case where providing subsidies to lower-income students to increase college enrollment satisfies both goals; we should strongly support those policies (Blinder, 1988).

These lessons from economics lay the groundwork for subsequent discussion. One critical issue regarding the effectiveness of price discrimination is that everyone needs to know that it is happening and understand the prices they face. Lower-income students cannot respond to the economic incentives of lower prices if they do not know they exist. Pricing transparency is a fundamental aspect of the success of such a system. Even with perfect information, though, the price that lower-income students face still may be too high. These topics are the focus of this book.

CHAPTER THREE

The Real Cost of College and Its Worth

Some officials interpret decline in the percentage of college-aged youths who are now attending college as sign that colleges have already begun to price themselves out of the American dream. (Peterson, 1973)

Access to higher education, a hallmark of an open society, is being threatened by rising college costs. (Hechinger, 1987)

As college costs have risen and Federal grants to needy students have declined over the last two decades, higher education has become significantly less affordable for students from poor families. (Honan, 1998)

The rising costs and limited grants are narrowing higher education's ability to serve as a bridge leading low-income and particularly minority youngsters into the middle class. (Schemo, 2001)

"If we go on this way for another 25 years, we won't have an affordable system of higher education," said Patrick Callan, president of the [National Center for Public Policy and Higher Education], a nonpartisan organization that promotes access to higher education. (Lewin, 2008)

As tuition and other fees have climbed and state funding of public institutions has failed to keep pace with rising costs and growing enrollment, a college education is being priced out of the reach of middle-class and even upper-middle-class families. (Finney, 2016)

A higher-education system that large portions of the population cannot afford would have devastating implications for that system, for the economy, and, perhaps most importantly, for social justice. That is why in this book I focus on how much college costs, what people know about it, and what to do about it.

Yet there must be something wrong with the way we think about the problem. Criticism regarding the high cost of college extends back at least fifty years. The arguments and language used over the past five decades have not changed much. College costs are too high, and our higher-educational system will collapse if they continue to spiral out of control.

Except that has not happened. Some will point to rising student debt as evidence of the growing problem; this is an issue I will address later in chapter 7. But the sky cannot be falling for fifty years.

Indeed, the percentage of recent high school graduates that enroll in college has increased from 50 percent in 1975 to 60 percent in 1990 and 70 percent in 2018 (Snyder, de Bray, and Brillow, 2019, table 302.10). More of that growth has occurred at the community college level, but around one-third of students who start out at a community college end up transferring to four-year institutions (Shapiro et al., 2017). Direct enrollment of recent high school graduates at four-year institutions has also risen over the past several decades (33 percent in 1975 to 40 percent in 1990 to 44 percent in 2018). Rising enrollment is puzzling if some students are being priced out of the market.

A piece of the puzzle is that all these expressions of rising costs focus on the sticker price. Those commenting on college costs rarely acknowledge the role played by the financial aid system and the fact that most students do not pay the sticker price. This chapter will clarify college costs for individuals with different levels of financial resources and at different types of academic institutions. What do these colleges actually charge their students? How have these actual costs changed over time? What can students from different financial backgrounds really expect to pay?

A college education also generates sizable private returns that need to be factored into any decision making as well. For higher-income students who pay the full sticker price, is college "worth it"? Does the answer depend on the type of institutions students attend? And what about for lower-income students? How does the availability of financial aid alter the rate of return to an investment in higher education? The purpose of this chapter is to answer these empirical questions.

What Do Colleges Charge?

The Goal

The starting point for this discussion is clarifying what we want to know: what does an individual student have to pay to attend college? We will also want a sense about whether the student can afford that price, and I will return to that topic in chapter 5, but we cannot get there without knowing what that student has to pay first.

That question is difficult to answer because most students pay a different price. I documented in chapter 1 that very few students actually pay the sticker price, so we need to take into account who is paying what. How much does a student whose family makes $50,000 per year pay? What about one whose family makes $100,000 or $200,000 per year? In reality, assets matter as well, so what we really want to know is how much does a student with, say, family income of $50,000 and assets valued at $75,000 really pay? How much do other families with different financial circumstances pay? That is the goal.

What Do We Know?

The data on college costs that are publicly available generally do not focus on prices that students with different individual financial circumstances pay. They focus on average statistics—what does the average student pay? Before advancing to a discussion of alternative statistics that analyze college pricing by specific family financial circumstances, I focus on the data that are publicly available and I provide thoughts on interpreting them.

The best available data on college costs come from the College Board, which routinely provides data on costs that distinguish sticker price from the price that students actually pay in its series Trends in College Pricing and Student Aid. Ma, Pender, and Libassi (2020) is the most recent example at the time this book was written. They disaggregate the analysis by type of institution, separating public from private and two-year from four-year institutions. They measure trends in cost of attendance (COA), including tuition, fees, and room and board, as well as other costs like travel, personal items, and books. They also construct a measure of these net costs of financial aid, which approximates average net price.

These data are a useful starting point. I extend their analysis here to focus more directly on COA and net price and to distinguish schools into the four categories on which I focus. These include public flagship/R1 institutions (including all flagships and other public universities with very high research activity—in California, Berkeley is the flagship and UCLA is R1), other public institutions, private institutions with large endowments, and other private institutions, all of which are nonprofit, four-year, and residential in nature. I use Integrated Postsecondary Education Data System

(IPEDS) data available from the National Center for Education Statistics (described in chapter 1) to conduct this exercise.

IPEDS data do not include the average net price that all students pay, just the average net price that students pay who receive financial aid. Data are available, though, on the percentage of students receiving financial aid. The average net price all students pay is the weighted average of the net price paid by those receiving aid and the COA for those not receiving aid. The percent receiving aid is the weight. As an example, suppose two-thirds of students received financial aid and their average net price was $20,000, and one-third of students received no financial aid and paid, on average, a $35,000 sticker price. The average net price that all students paid is $30,000 (= .67 × $20,000 + .33 × $35,000).

The most recent data available at the time this book was written are for 2017–18. Data necessary to describe net prices began being reported in 2008–9. I focus on the time period from 2008–9 through 2017–18 when I examine trends in these data. All dollar values are adjusted for inflation and are presented in 2018 dollars.

The results are presented in table 3.1 for selected years. The first panel of the table presents COA at the four different categories of institutions I consider. The institutions included in each category are the same over the years. The statistics reported within categories are not weighted by enrollment at each institution; my goal is to capture the nature of the institutions themselves, not what a typical student at these institutions might experience.

Over the past decade, the COA rose between 12 and 19 percent beyond inflation at these different types of institutions. These large price increases are consistent with the claims made at the beginning of this chapter about rising prices.

The rest of these data are presented in the next three panels of table 3.1. The second panel shows that average net prices paid by financial aid recipients are much lower than the sticker price—as a rough approximation across categories, they are half the value of the COA. This is an average, so some pay much less than that. This is the first indication that financial aid has a significant impact on reducing the cost of higher education in these data.

The average net price among financial aid recipients also rose more slowly than COA, rising by 3 to 9 percent across categories of institutions. This suggests that increases in sticker prices substantially exaggerate the price increase paid by financial aid recipients.

TABLE 3.1. Trends in alternative measures of college costs, selected years

Year	Public Flagship/R1	Other Public	High-Endowment Private	Other Private
		Average Cost of Attendance		
2008–9	$24,500	$21,100	$56,400	$41,500
2011–12	$26,200	$22,200	$59,300	$43,700
2014–15	$27,400	$23,400	$63,900	$46,400
2017–18	$27,800	$23,700	$66,900	$47,600
10-Year Change	$3,300	$2,600	$10,500	$6,100
10-Year % Change	13.3%	12.5%	18.6%	14.6%
		Average Net Price (if receiving aid)		
2008–9	$15,000	$13,000	$25,700	$23,700
2011–12	$15,400	$13,400	$26,600	$24,100
2014–15	$16,200	$14,000	$27,100	$24,700
2017–18	$16,200	$14,100	$27,100	$24,400
10-Year Change	$1,200	$1,100	$1,400	$700
10-Year % Change	8.2%	8.7%	5.3%	3.2%
		Average Percentage Receiving Grant Aid		
2008–9	64.8%	69.0%	67.5%	91.0%
2011–12	68.0%	74.0%	69.1%	93.4%
2014–15	69.6%	77.6%	69.3%	94.7%
2017–18	71.2%	80.4%	71.4%	95.9%
10-Year % Change	6.4%	11.4%	3.9%	4.9%
		Average Net Price (all students)		
2008–9	$18,400	$15,500	$36,800	$25,300
2011–12	$19,100	$15,800	$38,100	$25,400
2014–15	$19,800	$16,100	$39,800	$25,900
2017–18	$19,700	$16,000	$40,000	$25,500
10-Year Change	$1,300	$500	$3,200	$200
10-Year % Change	7.2%	2.7%	8.7%	0.4%

Source: Author's calculations based on data from IPEDS.
Note: All dollar values reflect inflation-adjusted (2018 dollar) average values across institutions within each category.

The third panel shows that the percentage of students receiving aid rose at each type of institution between 2008–9 and 2017–18. Across the different categories of institutions, the increase was 4 to 11 percentage points.

The final panel presents the average net price across all students by implementing the weighted average calculations. Increases in average net price differed across the different types of schools over this period. At public institutions below the flagship/R1 level and at private institutions that do not have large endowments, average net prices rose only slightly, by 2.7 percent and 0.4 percent, respectively, over the past decade. At public flagships and R1 institutions and high-endowment private institutions, though, average net prices rose 7.2 percent and 8.7 percent, respectively. These increases are still roughly half or less the size of the increases in the COA at these institutions.

Interpreting the IPEDS Data

There are some important issues embedded in these statistics from IPEDS data that require further discussion to interpret them correctly. To begin, consider price setting at institutions that meet full need. Of course, these institutions represent a minority of the market, and I will expand this discussion to other schools shortly, but this is a useful place to begin. At these institutions, families are charged their expected family contribution (EFC) (this ignores loans and work-study but incorporating those concepts would complicate the discussion for no benefit right now).

Figure 3.1 presents a stylized depiction of the distribution of EFCs in society. Many families have modest financial resources, and smaller and smaller numbers of people fall into the categories of families with higher and higher levels. This figure demonstrates an important statistical point— if the distribution has a shape like this, the mean (average) value of EFC will be larger than the median (the 50th percentile of the distribution) because the long right tail will pull up the mean, but not the median; Jeff Bezos increases average income, but not median income.

Now consider families with an EFC of $20,000 ($EFC_1$). If the COA is $30,000 ($COA_1$) at a meets-full-need school, those students will pay $20,000, not $30,000. If the COA rises to $35,000 ($COA_2$), or $40,000 ($COA_3$), that price increase does not change the cost to them. They still pay $20,000 because that is what they can afford based on their EFC.

Now consider other students with an EFC of $35,000 ($EFC_2$). From an initial COA of $30,000, those students pay the COA. If the COA increases to $35,000, they pay the full increase. But note that if the COA rises again to $40,000, those students do not pay the increase. They are now constrained by their EFC and continue to pay $35,000; that is what they can afford ($35,000, not $40,000).

These simple examples provide some valuable lessons about the impact of changes in the sticker price at institutions that meet full need. First, for many students those increases are meaningless; they do not affect them.

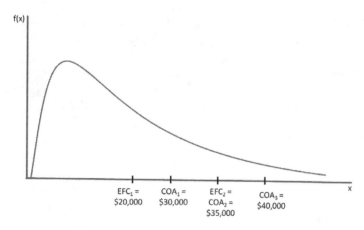

f(x)

EFC₁ =	COA₁ =	EFC₂ =	COA₃ =
$20,000	$30,000	COA₂ =	$40,000
		$35,000	

x

FIGURE 3.1. Impact of an increase in cost of attendance on financial aid receipt in a meets-full-need financial aid system

Second, for some students, an increase in the sticker price changes their eligibility for financial aid. The student with a $35,000 EFC became eligible for aid when the sticker rose from $30,000 originally to $40,000.

Third, when these additional students become eligible for financial aid, they pay more than the students who had been eligible for aid previously. The $20,000 EFC student was always in the pool of aided students. The $35,000 EFC student joined that pool in response to the sticker price increase from $35,000 to $40,000, increasing the average net price of aided students. Since there were likely many students already in that pool, the increase may be small, but the net price paid by aided students would rise following this sticker price change. That is a vestige of the changing sample of aided students and does not represent a true price increase among students already receiving financial aid.

For institutions that do not meet full need, the bottom line is similar. At those institutions, the net price can change when COA changes even for those already receiving financial aid. The $20,000 EFC student may be paying a net price of $25,000. If the sticker price rises from $30,000 to $35,000, that student's net price may rise as well. It is possible that this student would now pay $30,000 (increasing unmet need from $5,000 to $10,000), but the institution may also use some of the additional revenue to offset some of that burden for lower-income students. Suppose, for instance, this student's net price rose to $28,000. That would reflect a price increase for students receiving financial aid.

But it also would change the composition of the financial aid pool. The student with a $25,000 EFC who was originally paying the $30,000 sticker price would get swept into the pool of students receiving financial aid when the sticker price increased. Again, that would increase the average price paid for this group just by the change in composition. We need to take that into account in interpreting the data as well.

Figure 3.1 also provides an additional useful point in thinking about college pricing. When COA is low, an increase in the sticker price will generate a lot of revenue. All the students to the right of the COA in the figure will pay higher prices. When COA is high, however, an increase in the sticker price may generate less additional revenue. At that point, fewer students are paying the full sticker price, so the additional revenue obtained from a sticker price increase may be low. If the sticker price increase generates an increase in net price for students receiving financial aid, revenue can be enhanced, but that policy has an impact on lower-income students that may not be desirable.

This discussion helps interpret the statistics presented in table 3.1. The data show that the percentage of students who are receiving financial aid has been increasing, but this may not represent an increase in financial need or a change in college policy. It may simply be mechanical, resulting from the increase in COA. Continually adding in higher-income students will mechanically increase the average net price among aided students even if the price an individual student had to pay never changed. Also note that increases in the COA generate smaller increases in net prices at those types of institutions where more students receive financial aid.

Overall, what we learn from this analysis is that students typically pay less, and perhaps a lot less, than the sticker price. We also learn that a lot of students receive financial aid, and prices for those students are rising much more slowly than the COA. Finally, we learn that publicly reported statistics regarding college costs, like average COA and net price, may not be telling you what you think they are telling you.

The Concept of Individual Net Price

Rather than using aggregate statistics, a better way to measure cost is to measure what individual students with different financial characteristics would pay at different institutions. How much should a student with those finances expect to pay and how does that compare to the COA? How does that relationship change as finances change? How does that change over time (adjusted for inflation)? This is the best way to measure true college costs.

In theory, IPEDS data contain the necessary information to do this. Along with data on average net price among those eligible for financial aid, these data also contain the average net prices charged to students within a handful of income categories. The income categories include $30,000 or less, $30,001 to $48,000, $48,001 to $75,000, $75,001 to $110,000, and over $110,000.

These data have significant flaws, though (Levine, 2014). The simplest problem in these data is the use of an average rather than the median to say something about a typical student in each category. For instance, students in the lower-income bands are unlikely to be able to afford to pay much, if anything, toward college. But financial aid is based on income and assets, and some families have unusual financial circumstances with, say, very low income and not so low assets (a retiree?).

To confirm this, I used data from the 2016 Survey of Consumer Finances (SCF). The SCF is the premiere source of data on household finances, including both income and assets, in the United States. It is conducted every three years; 2016 is the most recent available data at the time I conducted this exercise while writing this book (the 2019 survey has been subsequently released).

According to my calculations from the 2016 SCF, 10 percent of families with children between the ages of thirteen and seventeen and incomes below $30,000 also have a net worth above $100,000. Seventeen percent of those with incomes between $30,000 and $48,000 have a net worth above $100,000. These families may not be able to afford much, but they can certainly afford more than they would based only on their income. Note that families with incomes below $50,000 do not need to report their assets on the FAFSA to receive federal aid, but they do on the CSS Profile and sometimes to receive institutional financial aid.

Since families with low incomes but greater assets are outliers, a simple solution to this problem would be to report statistics based on median net prices rather than average net prices. The median is a better indicator of a "typical" family when there are outliers. An average includes the net price paid by those families with those unusual finances. Outliers do not affect the median. This is an obvious flaw that needs to be corrected.

Another limitation of average net price data is that they ignore the large price differentials that students face depending on whether they have any siblings in college. Currently, a student's EFC is reduced by 40 or 50 percent (based on the formulas included in CSS Profile and FAFSA, respectively; recently enacted FAFSA simplification will eliminate the sibling discount) if a student has a single sibling concurrently enrolled. That translates to a significantly lower net price. The average net price students face aggregates students into a single pool, overlooking these large differences in pricing. Average net price data for students with no siblings concurrently enrolled are not publicly available to address this issue.

Simulating Individual Net Price

Again, it would be better to estimate the cost of attending different institutions or to compare changes in costs over time for students with set financial characteristics, including both income and assets. That would enable us to determine differences in financial aid policies across institutions as distinct from changes in student composition. No easy way of conducting this exercise exists now, though.

Instead, I simulate this approach using data from the 2016 SCF, described earlier, and government-mandated net price calculators (NPCs) at randomly selected institutions in each category. I focused on families in the SCF with children between the ages of thirteen and seventeen when the survey was conducted. Almost one thousand such families are included in these data.

I used those data to identify the most common forms of a family's financial holdings that matter in the financial aid process (which means I ignore retirement funds). These include nonretirement financial investments (like stock and bond holdings outside of retirement accounts), cash holdings, and home equity. I did not identify every possible form of asset that could be entered (detailed real estate, trusts, farm value, etc.), but the most common forms, which are more likely to appear on many NPCs.

Home equity (equal to a home's purchase price less any outstanding mortgage payments) is included in financial aid calculations based on the College Board's institutional methodology (IM) embedded in the CSS Profile, but not the federal methodology (FM) based on the FAFSA (see chapter 1 for more discussion on this distinction). I examined asset holdings with and without home equity, since NPCs based on IM will include it and others based on FM will not. Since it is a common form of asset and it matters at some institutions, I include it here.

Table 3.2 displays the values of income and assets at the 10th, 25th, 50th, 75th, and 90th percentiles of the income and asset distributions for these

TABLE 3.2. Income and asset values for families with children between the ages of thirteen and seventeen

Percentile	Total Family Income	Nonretirement Investments, Cash in the Bank, and Home Equity	Nonretirement Investments and Cash in the Bank (Excludes Home Equity)
10th	$19,900	$6,100	$5,000
25th	$36,600	$22,800	$13,900
50th	$70,100	$98,500	$36,300
75th	$119,300	$259,300	$128,600
90th	$210,300	$856,900	$563,700

Source: Author's calculations based on data from the 2016 Survey of Consumer Finances.
Note: Statistics are based on families with children between the ages of thirteen and seventeen and are population weighted. All statistics reflect inflation-adjusted (2018 dollar) values.

families in 2016, the year of the most recent SCF at the time I conducted this exercise. Since the financial aid system relies on lagged family finances, this survey year lines up nicely with the 2017–18 net price data reported earlier from IPEDS, displayed in table 3.1.

I then inserted these values into NPCs at a subsample of two hundred higher-educational institutions in the summer of 2020, randomly selecting fifty in each of the four categories I have been using. The task of obtaining an estimate from these tools is sufficiently cumbersome that conducting this exercise for all 1,315 schools that I examine is too formidable a hurdle. For those schools selected, I made the simplest possible set of assumptions regarding other information required beyond finances (dependent student, married parents, living on campus, no siblings, state residents, average tax liability given income level—obtained from the IRS, *Statistics of Income*). For institutions that provide merit awards, I used the 75th percentile SAT/ACT score at the institution (if test scores were requested on the NPC to be considered for merit), available from IPEDS, and assumed a 3.67 GPA. This is a high GPA, but I chose it to allow for at least a reasonable chance of a merit award at most institutions. All other requested information, if required, was based on judgment using plausible values.

Indeed, just conducting this exercise for two hundred institutions drove home a point that has been made previously by others, including the Institute for College Access and Success (2012); current NPCs are not always that helpful to families trying to better understand college costs. Problems identified just after NPCs were introduced almost a decade ago still exist today: difficulty finding an institution's NPC, difficulty understanding what information it was asking for, difficulty interpreting the results, failure to report other components of financial aid awards like loans and work-study, and other issues. I discuss these issues in more detail in chapter 4.

Despite these limitations and potential errors that may have been introduced because of the complexity, taking averages across institutions within a specific category is likely to yield insight into patterns in net prices. An important advantage of using these data is that they represent what colleges and universities themselves communicate to prospective students regarding their individualized cost.

The results of this analysis are reported in table 3.3 and figure 3.2. The top of the table displays the average stated COA (sticker price) within each category of schools among the two hundred included in this analysis. These values are very similar to those presented in table 1.4 for the full sample of institutions used. The next panel of table 3.3 and figure 3.2 present the results of our net price exercise using institutions' NPCs, reporting average net price across institutions within a category for each income/asset percentiles chosen. These estimates not only provide the benefit of overcoming differences in sample composition, but they also enable us to examine how net prices change as a student's financial resources change.

These calculations document the fact that the financial aid system reduces the price of attending college below the sticker price for almost all students; the price reduction is substantial for those from lower-income families. For instance, at public flagship institutions that charge a sticker price around $30,000, on average, students in the bottom quartile of the income distribution would pay a net price (including loans and work-study)

TABLE 3.3. Individual net prices charged to students, by type of institution and level of income and assets

	Public Flagship/R1	Other Public	High-Endowment Private	Other Private
Cost of Attendance	$29,200	$22,800	$67,500	$48,600
Income/Assets		Individual Net Price		
10th Percentile	$12,100	$12,000	$9,300	$19,900
25th Percentile	$14,300	$13,300	$10,700	$21,600
50th Percentile	$21,400	$18,700	$18,100	$25,800
75th Percentile	$25,700	$19,700	$33,500	$32,800
90th Percentile	$26,400	$20,000	$58,000	$35,600

Source: Author's calculations based on data from the 2016 Survey of Consumer Finances (see table 3.2) applied to net price calculators from a subsample of 200 institutions (50 in each category), randomly selected from the 1,315 schools in the full IPEDS dataset used elsewhere. All statistics, including COA, were obtained from this exercise, which was conducted in the summer of 2020.

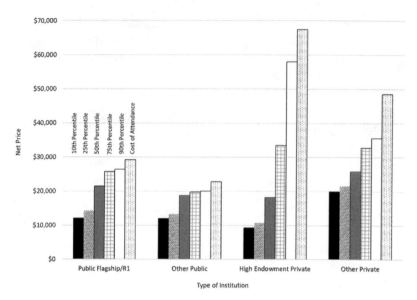

FIGURE 3.2. Net price gradient by income/asset percentile

of less than half that amount. Chapter 5 will address whether even these reduced prices are affordable, but these data highlight the mistake that students make if they focus on the sticker price.

Beyond that, one pattern that we see clearly in figure 3.2 is that the slope of this relationship is much steeper at high-endowment private colleges. At these institutions, a student at the 10th percentile of the income/asset distribution pays a net price of around $9,300 (including loans and work-study). This jumps to $58,000 at the 90th percentile. That is a jump in price of $48,700. At other public institutions (not flagship/R1), the 10th percentile family pays $12,000 and that jumps by $8,000 to $20,000 at the 90th percentile. This profile is much flatter. The slope for public flagship/ R1 institutions and other private institutions is only slightly steeper than that, largely because the sticker price is higher.

These patterns are consistent with the discussion presented in chapter 2 discussing the role of markets and competition in determining college pricing. I explained that private institutions with large endowments face the least competition and the most market power and can charge students from higher-income families a much higher price. This frees up resources that combine with endowment spending to offer much lower prices for lower-income students.

Public institutions are constrained by the state-established, relatively low maximum COA, which reduces prices for students from higher-income families. The diminished revenue this system generates reduces institutions' ability to maintain low prices for lower-income students. The net price profile is relatively flat.

Competition between public institutions and private institutions without large endowments means that the latter category cannot have a pricing system that is far out of line with public institutions. This restricts the amount of financial aid available at these institutions.

Overall, these data are difficult to come by, requiring extensive effort to compile, but they do a better job of capturing what students actually pay at different types of institutions than other data sources. Unfortunately, I have no way of identifying trends in costs this way (institutions only maintain current net price calculators, not historical versions; going forward, my calculations can be used as a starting point to evaluate future trends). What we can conclude, though, is that lower-income students pay considerably less than the sticker price.

One other limitation of this exercise is that it does not incorporate the provisions of the tax code that can further reduce the cost of college for many students, mainly through the American Opportunity Tax Credit. That credit is worth up to $2,500, $1,000 of which can be paid out directly to families with no tax liability (i.e., a refundable credit); its main beneficiaries are those with adjusted gross incomes of $30,000 to $180,000 (the eligibility limit for married parents filing jointly; Crandall-Hollick, 2018). For the present purposes, one could imagine subtracting $2,500 from the cost figures presented in table 3.3 for those in the 50th and 75th percentiles of the income and asset distributions. Those in the 10th and 25th percentiles are more likely to be eligible for the $1,000 refundable part of the credit. I have chosen to omit those values in the formal figures presented here.

Is College Worth It?

College is an investment decision, and choosing to attend should depend not only on the cost but also on the return. As an economist, I think of this as a question of whether the benefits are greater than the costs. In the language of admissions professionals, this is called the "value proposition." For everyone else, it is about whether college is "worth it." The benefits include intellectual fulfillment, personal growth, and personal connections, among other things, but usually when people ask whether college is worth it, they generally mean monetarily: do the higher earnings cover the cost of going to college? This discussion will focus on the earnings gain associated with attending college, recognizing that it is just part of the picture.

Whether college is worth it has gotten a lot of attention in recent years. A simple Google search asking the question will generate numerous links. A 2017 NBC News/*Wall Street Journal* poll (reported in Dann, 2017) found that about the same percentage of respondents indicated that college was worth it relative to those who felt it was not (49 percent relative to 47 percent). This compares to a similar CNBC poll conducted in 2013, which found a more pronounced belief in the value of college (53 percent relative to 40 percent). In the 2017 poll, a majority of those with white, working-class backgrounds and those who have not attended or completed college reported that college is not worth it. The premise of the question is based on the high cost of college, without factoring in the benefits (Kerr, 2019).

It turns out, of course, that this is not a question of opinion, but an empirical statement that we can answer. It involves the comparison of costs that are incurred today against the potential benefits that accrue over the remainder of the student's working life. I have provided extensive detail regarding costs already, but I have not yet focused on the benefits. The purpose of this discussion is to address those issues and then to provide more formal answers to the question of whether college is worth it.

The Benefits of College

At first glance, it may seem like the answer to this question is obvious. It is not surprising that college graduates make more money than those who do not have a college degree, and it is straightforward to document. In the first quarter of 2020 (US Bureau of Labor Statistics, 2020), median earnings for individuals with a college degree (but no advanced degree beyond that) who work full time earned $1,263 per week ($65,676 per year). Someone who worked the same amount with a high school degree only had earnings of $768 per week (around $39,936 per year). Taking the ratio of the medians, a full-time worker with a college degree makes 64.4 percent more than the same worker with a high school degree.

Why do they make more? A basic principle in economics is that workers are paid according to the revenues that their work brings in, which is related to how much they produce. One view is that college-educated workers make more because they are more productive. In the language of economics, college improves their "human capital." Human capital is a term that is linked to the notion of physical capital, like a machine. A machine is something expensive that requires a firm to make an investment decision. The firm pays a large sum of money now, and it improves the firm's productivity for some lengthy period. Human capital is a similar concept except that we make these investments in ourselves that improve our productivity. Work experience is one common example of a human capital investment that leads to higher subsequent wages. Additional education, including going to college, is another.

But here is the problem: students who attend and graduate from college may earn more because they are inherently more productive workers. They may have better problem-solving and time-management skills, for instance. These are attributes that employers like because workers who have them are likely to be more productive. Colleges may just be selecting students on the same basis as employers. If those students entered the labor market after high school, perhaps they would make higher wages anyway. In economics terminology, the college wage premium may be attributed to "selection bias," not an improvement in the worker's productive capacity.

If the college wage premium is associated with selection, this complicates the policy implications of promoting college attendance. If we encourage students to attend college who would not do so otherwise, selection bias suggests they will not receive higher wages; college does not change the person. They would still enter the labor market without the higher levels of productivity that employers seek in return for higher pay. If, for instance, they learn the time-management and problem-solving skills, though, those represent human capital investments that generate greater labor market returns. Does the college wage premium reflect an increase in human capital or selection? Promoting college attendance requires that the answer to this question is human capital.

Considerable research attention has been dedicated to determining whether obtaining more education has a "causal impact" on a worker's wages. Does attending college "cause" workers to earn more? In other words, does it increase their human capital? The causal effect of more education contrasts with the selection effect of more education. If the effect is causal and we encourage more people to go, they will receive higher earnings.

The main takeaway from this research is that there is ample reason to believe that a college education improves workers' human capital, and that is why their earnings are higher. It is beyond the scope of this book to review that evidence and the methodologies designed to draw that conclusion, but the interested reader should refer to Card (1999) or Oreopoulos and Petronijevic (2013).

Briefly, though, the goal is to find examples where two groups of students are otherwise identical except that one had the opportunity to receive an additional year of education just due to "luck." For instance, students who are young for their grade based on legislated school starting policies (typically those born in late August), obtain more education than students who are old for their grade (typically those born in early September). This occurs because, on average, they are in a higher grade when they reach the age at which compulsory schooling laws allow them to leave school. That additional year of education for those born in August leads to higher wages compared to those born in September, on average. In pairs of identical twins, the one who stays in school longer earns more. Students who happen to live very close to a community college are more likely to attend; they earn more than those who live farther away. Those are examples of the methods used to determine that additional education really alters a student's earnings. It is not just selection.

Earlier we saw that in 2020, college graduates earn 64.4 percent more than high school graduates. That amounts to a 13.2 percent increase in wages for every additional year of education over four years. This rate of return is roughly consistent with previous estimates of the causal impact. Based on Zimmerman (2014), Hershbein, Kearney, and Pardue (2020) similarly use an estimate of 68 percent as the causal impact on earnings associated with obtaining a college degree relative to a high school degree. For simplicity, I will continue to use the 64.4 percent figure.

The next step is to simulate lifetime earnings incorporating this wage premium, since it will continue throughout a worker's life. The appropriate technique to do so is called a net present value calculation. Since money in the future is worth less than it is today (would you rather have $100 today or 10 years from now?), we need to "discount" future sums to what they would be worth to us today. This approach requires us to set an interest rate—the rate at which that money would grow if we invested it conservatively—to determine how much money we would need today to generate a future dollar value. I use a 3 percent annual inflation-adjusted interest rate (also known as the "real" interest rate), which is reasonable and common assumption to make based on typical conditions in financial markets. One dollar today would be worth $1.03 next year, which means that you would only need $0.97 today for your money to grow to $1 next year. In other words, $1 next year is worth $0.97 today.

A high school graduate who currently earns $768 per week and works 52 weeks per year makes $39,936 per year. If the high school graduate keeps earning at the same rate, and we assume that $1 next year is only worth $0.97 today, then what would his equivalent annual earnings be next year, and the year after that? I calculate the equivalent amount for each year between now (when the high school graduate is eighteen) and retirement (at age sixty-five). By adding all those years together, we can estimate how much that high school graduate will earn over the course of his lifetime. This amount is called the net present value of lifetime wages, and for the high school graduate, it totals $1.04 million.

We can conduct a similar exercise for college graduates. For that student, the wage stream starts at age twenty-two and amounts to $1,263 per week for 52 weeks per year ($65,676 per year) through age sixty-five. That total also needs to be discounted back to age eighteen to make a fair comparison with the high school graduate. Note that college graduates are assumed to earn nothing for four years while they are in college, reducing the net present value of their lifetime wages. These discounted earnings total $1.46 million. In the end, college graduates make $420,000 more over their lifetimes in present discounted value terms (all in real terms—adjusted for inflation).

Comparing Benefits and Costs

College costs are considerably less than that. We saw in table 1.4 that the median four-year, residential, highly endowed private college has a sticker price of around $71,000 per year, or $268,000 over four years performing the same net present value calculation. Even at that price, college is an excellent investment. The $268,000 in costs generate higher lifetime income of $420,000. All other categories of college cost considerably less than that even for students paying full price. For a student paying the $27,000 sticker price at a state flagship university, the net present value of total college costs is roughly $115,000, an even lower amount relative to the additional $420,000 earned in wages over the course of a lifetime. Even at full price, college really is a good investment.

It is an even better investment for students receiving financial aid, which most students do. Note that the labor market does not know who paid how much for college. There is no reason to assume that a student receiving financial aid would earn any less than any other student attending college. In table 3.3, I show that a student with median values of financial resources pays $18,100 to attend a highly endowed private college. The net present value of those annual costs over four years is around $70,000. The wage premium associated with college attendance is far greater than that. And lower-income students face even a larger benefit-cost ratio than that. For students receiving financial aid, college is definitely worth it.

It may be more worth it depending on what you choose to study in college, though. Providing detailed data on the wages of students depending on these choices has been a policy goal for the past decade and considerable progress has been made. These data have been available for several years, including from Hershbein and Kearney (2014). Now students can access this information from the College Scorecard (https://collegescore card.ed.gov/). These data document that those who major in engineering make more than those who major in early childhood education, for instance. One needs to keep in mind, though, that the selection issues that are embedded in these data are more severe than they are in more aggregated data, as students choose what to study. Engineering majors have technical abilities that are likely to earn them higher wages anyway.

Research supports the view that choice of major does have a meaningful, causal impact on subsequent wages (Kirkeboen, Leuven, and Mogstad, 2016). This means that the major individuals choose will affect the rate of return they receive from attending college.

Is College Worth It for Everyone?

The evidence just presented on the value of a college investment is strong, but does that mean it is a good investment for everyone? There are some additional factors to take into consideration to answer that question.

The first is recognizing the difference between the characteristics of an average college student and a student who is on the fence about attending college. The preceding calculation is based on averages. On average, a college-educated worker makes a lot more than a worker with a high school degree. But students who attend college are different in many dimensions than students who do not, and some of those differences may impact the human capital improvements that a college education provides. Suppose there is an entire distribution of students who vary according to their potential benefit from attending college. The ones with the largest benefits may already be going, and the ones who are not currently attending may have smaller benefits. If we are to induce additional students to attend college, the relevant question is, What is the benefit for the next one who decides to enroll (in economics jargon, the "marginal" student)? That may not be as high as it is for the average student who would have gone to college anyway. Past research has shown, however, that the marginal student still receives a large return to attending college (Zimmerman, 2014; Smith, Goodman, and Hurwitz, 2020).

Discussion

The typical starting point in a conversation about college costs is the sticker price. It is not difficult to document, though, that the sticker price is not the relevant price for most of the population. The amount students end up paying is typically considerably less than that. Misinformation regarding the true cost colors much of the discussion regarding what college costs. And college is definitely "worth it," with returns that are considerably greater than its cost. For students receiving financial aid, those returns can far exceed the cost of their education.

If college is such a good investment, why is there a need to intervene in this market at all? If there were a well-functioning credit market, individuals should be able to borrow to make investments that are likely to pay off. But the ability of students to obtain that sort of credit may be restricted, and students may be averse to take on that level of debt anyway, limiting this potential solution to the problem (Lochner and Monge-Naranjo, 2012).

Moreover, it is also difficult for students to make rational investment decisions when they do not fully understand the costs and benefits that they face. Misinformation regarding costs is rampant, as I will document in the next chapter, and that alters the decisions that individuals make regarding their education. This needs to be addressed. For some students, though, the problem is not the information about the cost; it really is the cost. This issue is primarily relevant for students from lower-income families, who may not be able to afford the price even in the presence of financial aid. Chapter 5 documents that issue.

CHAPTER FOUR

Pricing Transparency

Think about markets other than higher education where price discrimination occurs, meaning that firms (legally) use their market power to charge different prices to different groups of consumers based on likely willingness to pay. In chapter 2, I discussed airline pricing as an example of this. How do people know how much they will pay? In simple examples, like the pricing of movie tickets, everyone has come to expect that tickets to matinees will cost less than tickets to evening showings. But that is just two prices based on the time of the show, so it is not that hard for the information to disseminate. As the extent of price discrimination in a market increases, determining and communicating the price that an individual will actually pay becomes more difficult.

We do have examples, though, of more complex systems of price discrimination where individuals can easily determine their cost. Airline pricing is one of them. Pricing for seats on a plane from point A to point B vary considerably. The underlying algorithm that airlines use to generate those prices are complex, and consumers certainly are not privy to all of those details. More sophisticated travelers know (or think they know) some of the basics, though. Flying on Tuesday and Wednesday is generally cheaper, and flights around major holidays, like Thanksgiving, are more expensive.

Yet we also know that the exact fare we will have to pay includes components that we are unlikely to perfectly forecast. Airlines solve the problem with very simple-to-use web pages that require travelers to enter basic information of when and where they are looking to travel. One can check at jetblue.com, united.com, delta.com, or any airline's website to check prices. Within a few seconds, the pricing tool provides results. Uber is another example where technology facilitates the dissemination of differential pricing. Those pricing systems work. Few people who would have liked to fly or get a ride avoid doing so because they cannot figure out what the price will be (although my mother-in-law does have some difficulty with Uber!).

The system of communicating differential prices in higher education does not work so well. It is complicated and far from transparent. The information gaps generated by such a confusing system are not difficult to document with survey evidence, which I will present below. These problems are obvious to anyone who has gone through the process (including me). In a market where perfect price discrimination not only exists but is socially desirable; failure to clearly transmit what students will really have to pay after factoring in financial aid is a serious issue.

How did we get to a point where the system of college pricing simply does not work? What is the history of financial aid that has made it so complicated that no one can understand it? What attempts have been made to address the problem, and why have they not been successful? How has the confusion regarding college pricing affected prospective students' college-going decisions? Where should we go from here? These are the questions that I will address in this chapter.

Documenting Lack of Knowledge Regarding College Pricing

In looking at survey data regarding college costs among prospective students and their families, the first thing to note is the level of concern that they express. People believe that college is too expensive. Over the past several years, Gallup has conducted polls asking random samples of American adults whether "education beyond high school is affordable for anyone in this country who needs it?" (Markin, 2020). The most recent poll, conducted in 2019, indicates that 73 percent say that it is not. This rate is virtually unchanged since 2012.

In chapter 3, though, I provided estimates of how much colleges actually charge, after factoring in financial aid, for students whose families are at several points in the distributions of income and assets. That analysis showed that the net price of attending all types of higher-educational institutions is considerably less than the sticker price. That does not necessarily make it affordable; that is the focus of the next chapter. But the cost may be less than people think.

Survey evidence supports this view. Results from a 1997–98 survey of parents showed that they overestimated the actual cost of attending college by 100 percent at four-year public institutions (in state) and 40 percent at four-year private institutions (Ikenberry and Hartle, 1998). A 1999 survey showed that almost 30 percent of students in grades 11 and 12 and their parents overestimated the cost of attending college (Horn, Chen, and Chapman, 2003). Roughly the same percentage could not even provide an estimate.

The problem has not improved over time, despite policies introduced to help overcome it (described below). One 2015 survey found that parents overestimated the net price by 50 percent at four-year private institutions and 85 percent at four-year public institutions (Bleemer and Zafar, 2018), almost identical to survey responses two decades earlier. Parents of students in ninth grade similarly estimated net tuition (not including room and board) to be roughly twice as much as what it actually costs (Velez and Horn, 2018). Only 12.9 percent of those parents were very confident in their estimates.

One reason why families may overestimate the cost of college is because the only cost figure they know is the sticker price. Survey evidence supports this proposition. One survey of high school seniors in late 2009 / early 2010 found that 59 percent only considered the sticker price without considering the availability of financial aid. A follow-up survey showed that the focus on sticker price was even greater among lower- and middle-income students than more affluent students (Hesel and Meade, 2012). Yet a third follow-up survey found perhaps some improvement by 2015, but still almost half of high school seniors were only looking at sticker prices in thinking about college costs (Hesel, Camara, and Kappler, 2015).

History of Federal Legislation Regarding College Pricing

Sometimes policy is designed with the best of intentions, but relatively small flaws in implementation significantly diminish its impact. Laws governing college costs and financial aid fall into this category. Aspects of public policy have both contributed to the confusion regarding college costs and attempted to resolve it, albeit unsuccessfully.

One example is the federal requirement that each school report its cost of attendance (COA). As I described briefly in chapter 1, the 1965 Higher Education Act was the first piece of federal legislation to broadly provide financial assistance to pay for college. At that point, helping students amounted to providing loans. Students from families with incomes below $15,000 (roughly $120,000 in 2020 dollars) could borrow up to $1,000 (roughly $8,000 in 2020 dollars) at subsidized rates. That was the main component of federal financial aid at that point.

It was the 1972 amendment to the Higher Education Act, though, that introduced the issue of COA. That legislation introduced the Basic Educational Opportunity Grant, which was renamed the Pell Grant in 1980. The law instituted a formula that a student would be eligible for a benefit equal to $1,400 minus the student's expected family contribution (EFC). The maximum benefit remained at $1,400 (around $6,500 in 2020 dollars) through the mid-1970s (Mahan, 2011). Importantly, the law also stipulated that the "amount of a basic grant to which a student is entitled under this subpart for any academic year shall not exceed 50 per centum of the actual cost of attendance at the institution at which the student is in attendance for that year" (Education Amendments of 1972, 20 U.S.C. § 1070 [1973]; current version at 20 U.S.C. § 1070).

And that is where the problem started. As stated in chapter 1, the law went on to define the actual COA as "the actual per-student charges for tuition, fees, room and board (or expenses related to reasonable commuting), books, and an allowance for such other expenses as the Commissioner determines by regulation to be reasonably related to attendance at the institution at which the student is in attendance" (Education Amendments of 1972, 20 U.S.C. § 1070 [1973]; current version at 20 U.S.C. § 1087).

However, that is not the actual COA. It is the maximum COA—the sticker price. It is true that more students paid the maximum COA in 1972 than do so today. One factor that can explain this is that sticker prices rose faster than incomes. As I documented in chapter 1, though, few students pay that maximum cost now.

The maximum COA is a useful number for the purposes of calculating financial aid. It would be difficult to justify providing more financial assistance beyond that value. But if that is the only number that prospective students know or can easily access, it provides a very misleading picture of what college costs. It does a poor job of representing the actual cost of college.

Yet this sticker price is typically the easiest number to find regarding how much it would cost a student to attend an institution. The Higher Education Act requires that the COA be disseminated through "appropriate publications, mailings, or electronic media" (National Postsecondary Education Cooperative, 2009). In effect, the most accessible piece of information available regarding college costs is one that almost certainly overstates what students would have to pay. A simple relabeling of the term from *COA* to *maximum COA* could help. It would at least alert students to the fact that they may pay less than the sticker price.

Besides the labels used, the process of calculating financial aid awards and the complexity involved further confuses students and their families. The concept of using a formula to calculate an EFC is one that goes back to the 1950s, when John Monro, director of financial aid at Harvard University at that time, proposed the first version of "needs analysis" (Halberstam, 1953). His formula for the EFC could not have been much simpler (National Association of Student Financial Aid Administrators, 2014). It was based solely on after-tax income and the number of children in a family attending public or private school (K-12):

$$EFC = 0.15 \times \text{net income} - 100 \times \text{children (public school)}$$
$$- 200 \times \text{children (private school)}.$$

Since then, several different, often competing, formulas have been implemented, becoming considerably more complex. The 1972 law that introduced the Basic Educational Opportunity Grant required such a formula since benefits were set as the maximum level less a student's EFC. FAFSA was introduced in 1992 to determine eligibility for federal financial aid. Just afterward, the College Board launched the CSS/Profile (Wilkinson, 2005), which is used mainly by private institutions. Those schools sought a tool that would provide more detail regarding the financial details of applicants, including home equity and the finances of noncustodial parents, offering a better measure of a student's ability to pay to inform their financial aid awards. Students seeking financial aid at one of the roughly four hundred schools that rely on the CSS Profile still need to complete the FAFSA to be eligible for federal financial aid. Other financial aid forms and formulas have existed along the way. Today, just the fact that there are two competing systems creates confusion.

Then we get to the questions that they ask. There are 103 questions on the FAFSA. Yes, 103 questions. Many of them are easy to answer (like basic demographics), but others are not. For instance, question 92 asks about untaxed income. This question is designed to measure "cash flow" more precisely to better assess how much parents can afford to pay. But the question itself has eight subsections, *a* through *h*. Here is what the 2020–21 form asks for:

92. Parents' 2018 Untaxed Income (Enter the amounts for your parent[s]).

a. Payments to tax-deferred pension and retirement savings plans (paid directly or withheld from earnings), including, but not limited to, amounts reported on the W-2 forms in Boxes 12a through 12d, codes D, E, F, G, H and S. Don't include amounts reported in code DD (employer contributions toward employee health benefits).

b. IRA deductions and payments to self-employed SEP, SIMPLE, Keogh and other qualified plans from IRS Form 1040 Schedule 1—total of lines 28 + 32.

c. Child support received for any of your parents' children. Don't include foster care or adoption payments.

d. Tax exempt interest income from IRS Form 1040—line 2a.

e. Untaxed portions of IRA distributions and pensions from IRS Form 1040—line 4a minus line 4b. Exclude rollovers. If negative, enter a zero here.

f. Housing, food and other living allowances paid to members of the military, clergy and others (including cash payments and cash value of benefits). Don't include the value of on-base military housing or the value of a basic military allowance for housing.

g. Veterans noneducation benefits, such as Disability, Death Pension, or Dependency & Indemnity Compensation (DIC) and/or VA Educational Work-Study allowances.

h. Other untaxed income not reported in items 92a through 92g, such as workers' compensation, disability benefits, untaxed foreign income, etc. Also include the untaxed portions of health savings accounts from IRS Form 1040 Schedule 1—line 25. Don't include extended foster care benefits, student aid, earned income credit, additional child tax credit, welfare payments, untaxed Social Security benefits, Supplemental Security Income, Workforce Innovation and Opportunity Act educational benefits, on-base military housing or a military housing allowance, combat pay, benefits from flexible spending arrangements (e.g., cafeteria plans), foreign income exclusion or credit for federal tax on special fuels.

Perhaps it is unwise of me to state this directly, but I think the reader will agree with me: this is ridiculous. What are "Boxes 12a through 12d, codes D, E, F, G, H and S" on the W-2 form (and what form is that?), and why should I not include "amounts reported in code DD (employer contributions toward employee health benefits)"? Does anyone really know what the "Workforce Innovation and Opportunity Act educational benefit" is? If you cannot understand the questions, you cannot easily answer them, and you certainly cannot forecast the result. Imagine how difficult it is for students with less-educated parents or for those who are not required to complete tax forms.

In defense of the FAFSA, at least the questions are posted online along with the formula that is used to compute EFC. If you were a tax attorney, perhaps you could figure it out. The CSS Profile questionnaire is only available after logging in to their system. The formulas they use are proprietary. FAFSA also has the advantage that one can complete part of the form by simply requesting to transfer the information on the tax forms you submit to the IRS directly to the FAFSA (see https://studentaid.gov /resources/irs-drt-text for instructions). Recent legislation enacted to simplify the FAFSA, described in chapter 6, will make this process of transferring income data easier once it goes into effect for college admissions in 2024. It is also slated to reduce the number of questions asked, but it is too early to know exactly what the form will contain.

Still, that may help when you complete the form, but it does not help if you want to know in advance how much college is going to cost. The advance knowledge that one can afford college is what is needed to take all the necessary steps to be in position to apply in the fall of your senior year (take the right courses, work hard to get good grades, investigate appropriate institutions, etc.). Waiting until October of the student's senior year is too late.

And even if the formula were as simple as the one John Monro introduced, it still only provides you with an estimate of EFC. That is all you need to determine your eligibility for a Pell Grant, but financial aid at most colleges and universities, and certainly most of those four-year residential institutions that are the focus of this study, provide other forms of financial aid beyond the Pell Grant. If the institution meets full financial need, then aid would be provided to fill in the gap between COA and EFC. That would include a Pell Grant. But most institutions do not meet full need. Knowing your EFC at those institutions does not help that much. How much of the gap between COA and EFC is the institution going to fill in? Nothing about this process enables us to answer that question.

To recap, the only easily identifiable cost figure is the (maximum) COA. The process used to determine eligibility for financial aid is overwhelming. Even if you knew the EFC, which is what financial aid formulas calculate, that does not provide you with enough information to figure out how much you will have to pay to attend a particular college. Is it really that surprising that families have such a difficult time estimating actual college costs and that they rely more heavily on the sticker price? Something is wrong here.

Attempts to Reform the System

This is not news to those who focus on public policy regarding higher education. The fact that researchers were conducting surveys asking people to estimate the cost of college decades ago indicates that they thought it might be a problem. Several innovations have been introduced in the past decade or so attempting to reduce the problem.

Some of these changes focus on making the process of completing the FAFSA easier and providing earlier estimates of the EFC. It used to be that students and their families could start to complete the FAFSA in January of the year in which they planned to enter college. That made sense if the income data used to calculate the EFC was from the past year; the year needed to end before all the information became available. Without completing the FAFSA, though, students had no estimate of their EFC and no knowledge of their eligibility for a Pell Grant. Institutions that based their financial aid awards on FAFSA could not generate financial aid awards. Students who were applying to college by, say, a January 1 admissions deadline would receive no information about their eligibility for financial aid until after they applied. Given the limited understanding of net prices, this information gap could inhibit applications.

To help address this problem, President Obama instituted an initiative in 2015 (White House, Office of the Press Secretary, 2015) that made two important changes. First, it moved up the availability of the FAFSA form to October of the preceding year. Second, it allowed families to use income data from the year before that (two years before college entry) to complete the form. This policy was called "prior-prior year." The College Board followed suit and introduced these policies as well for its CSS Profile financial aid form. The same executive order by President Obama also introduced the ability of families to transfer their tax data from the IRS directly to their FAFSA form, as described earlier. This is not possible for the CSS Profile.

These changes are clearly helpful, but they also represent minor advances in facilitating knowledge regarding financial aid and the ability to make more informed college decisions. They moved up the date from which a student can learn about their eligibility for a Pell Grant by a few months, perhaps even before they apply to college. Since most schools do not meet full need, though, students cannot find out a final financial aid award at an institution until after they apply to that school. These changes do not move forward final information regarding net price to predate the application period. They may make the process a bit easier and perhaps less stressful from a processing standpoint, but they cannot have a substantive impact on application decisions. For that to happen, students need better information regarding true college costs after factoring in financial aid months or years before they apply. These changes do not accomplish that.

President Obama also took steps to increase knowledge about colleges by introducing the College Scorecard in his 2013 State of the Union address. The College Scorecard is a website (https://collegescorecard.ed .gov/) that enables users to enter the name of a higher-education institution and easily obtain extensive data regarding its characteristics, including information on its curriculum, student body, and selectivity. It also includes information designed to make it easier for students to understand the value of attending that institution, including the graduation rate, salaries of graduates, loan default rates, and costs. The collection of these data was instituted in the 2008 Higher Education Opportunity Act (an amendment to the 1965 Higher Education Act) and included in a College Navigator website at that time that is still operational (https://nces.ed.gov/col legenavigator/). It is more detailed than the Scorecard, but the newer tool is more user friendly and marketed more heavily.

It is the cost component of this website that I will focus on here. The highlighted cost data presented represent the average net price paid by students at the institution. But as I discussed in chapter 3, the average net price is a statistic that captures both how expensive a school is and the composition of its students. Two institutions that would charge an individual applicant exactly the same amount may have substantially different average net prices if the financial status of their students differed. The school with a higher-income/asset student population would appear to be more expensive, and that comparison would be inaccurate.

Consider, for instance, two institutions with a $50,000 sticker price that both meet full need. At School A, half the students pay full price, and the other half have low incomes with a $10,000 net price. The average net price at School A would be $30,000. At School B, half the students also pay full price, but the other half have incomes and assets that generate a $20,000 net price. The average net price at School B would be $35,000. Both schools have exactly the same financial aid policies and sticker price, but the net price at School B is $5,000 higher. This is about the composition of the student body, not the pricing system.

The College Scorecard also provides average net price data for students with family incomes in five different income bands ($30,000 or under, $30,001–$48,000, $48,001–$75,000, $75,001–$110,000, and $110,001 or more). These data help address the problem that differences in student composition creates, but issues still remain in their interpretation. As I discussed in chapter 3, for instance, the use of averages rather than medians is a problem for a statistic that is affected by outliers. In this case, a family's asset holdings contribute to net price, and that distribution is heavily skewed. This bias similarly affects statistics on the average net price among all students (i.e., not by income category).

To demonstrate this statistical bias, I conduct an analysis comparing the average and median EFC. Net price is not the same as EFC, but the two concepts are strongly related. I use the same 2016 Survey of Consumer Finances data that I described in chapter 3 to obtain the finances of a sample of prospective college students. I restrict that sample to families with incomes below $110,000 (the income cutoff used by the College Scorecard). Then I apply an algorithm that is designed to mimic EFC calculations based on a family's financial information available in these data. In chapter 5, I use this approach extensively and describe this process in more detail there.

For these families with incomes below $110,000, median estimated EFC is $5,700, and mean estimated EFC is $9,200, a 61 percent higher estimate. This is what we would expect if some families have extreme asset values, which would increase the mean EFC, but not the median. This is a meaningful overstatement and one that is easily corrected by reporting the median rather than the mean.

The ultimate problem with the College Scorecard data, though, is that families want to know what college is going to cost them, not some average that they have difficulty relating to. Many institutions have reported average statistics on their own web pages for quite some time to no avail. Students do not believe average statistics. What they want to know is how much is college going to cost *me*? The College Scorecard does not provide that.

Federal legislation has attempted to address the issue of individualized estimates as well, but with limited success. The 2008 Higher Education Opportunity Act also included many provisions regarding the financial aid system; it increased the size of the Pell Grant and reduced interest rates on subsidized student loans, among other things.

For present purposes, though, the most important feature of that law was the introduction of net price calculators (NPCs). The stated purpose was to enable "current and prospective students, families, and consumers to determine an estimate of a current or prospective student's individual net price at a particular institution" (Higher Education Opportunity Act, 20 U.S.C. § 1015 [2018]). It is exactly the right idea.

But execution matters. NPCs have been criticized from almost the moment they were first introduced. The Institute for College Access and Success (2012) conducted an analysis a year after NPCs became mandatory in 2011 and reported substantial problems. They found that some NPCs were hard to find on school websites, hard to use, and provided confusing results. Several years later, Perna, Wright-Kim, and Jiang (2019) found the situation has not improved much.

My own exercise in chapter 3 found similar results. Again, I obtained net price estimates for families with five sets of financial characteristics (10th, 25th, 50th, 75th, and 90th percentiles of income and asset distributions for families with high school age students) for two hundred randomly selected four-year residential colleges and universities categorized into four groups (public flagship/R1, other public, high-endowment private, and other private).

Functionally, many of the NPCs worked reasonably well. They were relatively easy to find by going to a school's financial aid web page and then searching for their net price calculator. They provided estimates of net prices, sometimes along with other characteristics of the financial aid package (loan and work-study expectations) based on COA values from the current or past year. Many institutions provide merit awards, and an estimate of the value of those awards was provided as well. Those additional features were found in perhaps half of the NPCs.

But those features were not universal. Many schools based their awards on data that were out of date (two provided no indication of the date, and another reflected statistics for 2014–15; this exercise was conducted in June and July of 2020). Some schools required the user to leave their website to get additional information (like from the FAFSA4caster, which is an online tool the federal government operates to help forecast eligibility for federal financial aid) to calculate an EFC separately. Two asked about the race of the applicant. Three were nonfunctional over the several-week period over which I conducted this exercise. One of these was a very large public university with tens of thousands of students. Another flashed a warning that my connection to the website was not fully secure, which seems like a significant roadblock for a website that requires users to input their financial data.

Perhaps the weakest among them were those that relied on the Department of Education's NPC tool. Around one-quarter of the schools (mostly public institutions and more of these in the nonflagship/R1 category) used this tool. It is available to higher-education institutions for free. Other than demographics (family size, marital status, etc.), the only financial information required is income in $10,000 brackets up to $100,000 and then a separate category for $100,000 or more. Presumably, the resulting data are obtained from colleges reporting the mean net price within those income bands. As I have discussed earlier, though, there are limitations to that approach. It certainly ignores the variation in assets that exists across families that could help provide a more individualized estimate.

Aside from the Department of Education calculator, which asks virtually nothing about a family's finances, many other NPCs ask for financial information that may be difficult for individuals to answer. Financial tools that are designed to be easy to use need to avoid tax information. Most people do not like doing their taxes (and often use software like TurboTax or hire others to do it for them), and many do not fully understand foundational tax concepts. Asking them to provide information like their adjusted gross income, untaxed income, or "adjustments to income" is going to cause confusion and may prevent some from completing the process.

In my many conversations with financial aid professionals at colleges and universities that have typical NPCs, they comment on users' low completion rate. Users get to these questions that they cannot answer off the top of their heads and they stop. Digging out their tax forms to look up the correct answer is something they do not want to do. Simplicity must be a component of a well-designed NPC. They generally do not satisfy that principle.

Impact of Price Confusion on College-Going Decisions

If prospective students do not understand how much college is going to cost, and typically overestimate it (perhaps because they only know the sticker price), how are they supposed to make well-informed decisions regarding whether and where to go to college? Considerable research has been conducted over the past decade or so that is designed to answer exactly that question. The answer is that information matters. It may not be the only thing necessary to enable students to make better decisions regarding college, but it certainly helps.

How Can We Tell Whether Information Matters?

Before reviewing that research, it is useful to describe the standard of evidence that is necessary to draw conclusions along the lines that one thing "causes" another. A simple lesson from introductory statistics classes like the one I teach is that correlation is not the same as causation. In fact, on the first and last day of the semester, I reiterate that this is the most important lesson students will learn all semester. The fact that students who do not go to college are more likely to be misinformed about the price tells us nothing. Perhaps the students who have no interest in attending college do not seek out the information they would need to make an informed decision. The decision is already made.

The question we want to answer is, What would happen if we took a student who is not planning to attend college (or, perhaps, a certain type of college, like a four-year residential institution rather than a community college) and provided them with better information regarding the price? Would that change their decision? If so, that would be a causal effect of better pricing information on college-going behavior.

The most reliable way of proving a causal link between pricing transparency and college-going behavior is to implement a randomized controlled trial (RCT) evaluation of a pricing information intervention. We are likely all well versed in this approach lately because that is how vaccines, like the ones for COVID-19, are tested. The idea in the present context is to take a group of high school students and randomly assign some of them to a treatment group that has access to improved pricing and financial aid information and randomly assign others to a control group that experiences business as usual.

Random assignment guarantees that the treatment and control groups are statistically identical. Both have the "same" (in a statistical sense— i.e., no different than one would expect based on random variation) demographic characteristics, same parental education, same educational background themselves, and the like. These characteristics are all observable; even without an RCT, researchers can statistically adjust for any differences in these characteristics across students. An important benefit of random assignment, though, is that it also guarantees that the two groups are the same in ways that are more difficult for researchers to observe— same desire to attend college, same work ethic, same ability to navigate bureaucracy, and the like. The only difference between the two groups is the treatment—the college pricing information. If the treatment group enrolls in college (or a particular type of college) at a higher rate than the control group, it must be because of the treatment as opposed to differences in these hard-to-observe traits. That is a causal effect.

In real-world research, we are able on some occasions to introduce RCTs that operate exactly as I just described. Other times we exploit an intervention that affects one group of students but not others in a way that very much feels like it was random. This approach is sometimes called a quasi experiment or natural experiment. Although no formal randomization took place, we evaluate the outcome as if that were the case.

What Does the Evidence Show?

Regarding access to information about college pricing, we have several recent examples of these approaches to determine a causal effect (see Dynarski et al., 2021, for a thorough review of previous academic research on these issues). Some of this evidence finds strong support for the notion that providing more transparent and accessible pricing information has a large impact on college applications and enrollments. Hoxby and Avery (2013) document the existence of a large number of high-achieving (high SAT scores), lower-income students who end up attending nonselective institutions (like community colleges), labeled "undermatching." Hoxby and Turner (2013) report the results of an RCT designed to identify these students and then randomly assign a group of them to receive detailed information on the colleges that they have the potential to attend and the prices they are likely to face at those institutions after factoring in financial aid. The results indicate that students receiving the treatment were 56 percent more likely to apply to a "peer college" (i.e., one that is a better match for their academic abilities, again based on SAT scores), 78 percent more likely to be admitted to one of these schools and 46 percent more likely to enroll in one of them.

It is important to note that a more recent study conducted by the College Board found that a similar intervention had no broad impact on enrollments (Gurantz et al., 2019). This research effort also provided college information, including pricing, to a much larger sample of students; they were not able to find any large-scale effects of their intervention. The part of this analysis that was most closely comparable to that from Hoxby and Turner's study yielded similar but less precise results. They offer several possibilities for the different results, including a distaste for receiving direct information from the College Board, an organization that also interacts with students through the administration of AP and SAT exams.

In a different intervention, Dynarski et al. (2021) report the results of an RCT they conducted at the University of Michigan based on the introduction of a free-tuition policy called the "Hail Scholarship." They similarly focused on low-income, high-achieving students who tended to enroll in community colleges in Michigan rather than at the flagship institution in the state, where they would likely be strong candidates. Randomly selected, low-income students received prominent mailers (maize and blue!) telling them that they could attend the University of Michigan tuition free. Note that the offer did not cover the full COA (including room and board, for instance), just the tuition and fees component. Yet standard financial aid policies at the University of Michigan would enable any low-income student, regardless of the intervention, to attend tuition free. In fact, the financial aid package they would likely receive would also cover much of their other expenses regardless of the offer. The intervention is strictly about the information (which some might call marketing in this context). A second major element of the intervention is that those who received the "scholarship" offer did not need to complete the FAFSA to receive it.

These researchers found applications and enrollments jumped strongly for members of the treatment group relative to the control group. Recipients of the mailer were about two and a half times more likely to apply and enroll than others. The information mattered.

Still another RCT was conducted by Bettinger et al. (2012) that incorporated the assistance of H&R Block (the tax preparation service). Families with children approaching college age who sought help from the tax preparation service in completing their taxes were split into a control group and two treatment groups. In one of the treatments, families were told about their eligibility for federal financial aid after their taxes were completed along with information regarding local college options. In the second treatment, families received those services along with assistance completing the FAFSA. The results indicate that providing information alone had no statistically significant impact on college going, but the information provision along with assistance completing the FAFSA did. Enrollment rates jumped by around 25 percent for those receiving this treatment relative to the control group.

The final experiment I will review here is one conducted by Bleemer and Zafar (2018), assessing the role of pricing and the college returns on college-going expectations. Their analysis focuses on surveys of household heads with children under the age of eighteen. In one treatment, they provide respondents with information about average net prices of public and private nonprofit universities. In a second treatment, they provide information regarding the average college wage premium, which I documented in chapter 3. Respondents are asked both before and after these treatments whether they expect their children to attend college. The results indicate that parents provided with information about the returns to college are 4.9 percentage points more likely to say they expect their children to attend college. No statistically significant impact is observed for those receiving cost information. It is worthwhile to note that the cost treatment only provided average net price information to parents, not individualized estimates, which still may be too high for lower-income families, and that may have dampened its impact.

In my own research, my coauthors and I have investigated a quasi experiment brought about by the Great Recession (Levine, Ma, and Russell, 2020). At that time, sticker prices at all public flagship institutions rose considerably because state support dropped in response to declining state revenues. Some public flagships, though, meet full financial need (at that time, this group included Michigan, Virginia, UC Berkeley, and North Carolina). At those institutions, lower-income students were not subject to the tuition increase unless their incomes also rose, which was unlikely during the recession. Their application behavior should not have changed since the actual cost of attending college did not change for them. Students at other institutions and higher-income students living in these states with flagships that meet full need may have been expected to respond to the tuition increase by applying less frequently. This is the setup of the quasi experiment. We find that the lower-income students unaffected by the price increases still apply less often, just as much so as the other groups that were affected by the tuition increase. This is direct evidence of sticker shock. They did not know that those tuition increases did not affect them.

What can we conclude based on this research? Providing better information specific to individual families regarding college costs appears to have a meaningful potential to increase applications and enrollments of lower-income students. It may be that we need to do so alongside other support services, like financial aid application assistance, to achieve that outcome. The College Board experiment, which had limited effects, seems to be an outlier. Vastly simplifying the financial aid process in a way that obviates the need for application assistance could work as well. Students need to know the price they are going to pay, and they need to be able to complete the financial aid process so that they can pay it. That is what will help overcome the problems associated with the lack of pricing transparency.

Discussion

This example will date me, but I recall the introduction of MP3 players that enabled users to listen to music stored in electronic files on the device. They replaced portable CD players. When MP3 players were first introduced, many manufacturers made them, but none were particularly elegant or easy to use. Then Apple introduced the iPod and quickly dominated the industry with a device that had one button and an intuitive interface. Apple repeated that approach with the iPhone and other products, changing the way we live our lives.

In terms of financial aid, we are currently living in a world of MP3 players. We have tools that "work," but they are not elegant, and they certainly are not easy to use. If we are going to move forward, the financial aid system needs to do a much better job. A college education has the potential to provide significant economic benefit to students from lower-income families, and we are wasting the opportunity to enable them to receive those benefits. We are all better off as a society if students are able to take full advantage of their productive potential by enrolling in college or in an institution that is a better fit for them. We must find ways to simplify the system and easily communicate the price to take advantage of that.

CHAPTER FIVE

Addressing Affordability

For some students, imperfect information regarding costs is not the problem; the actual high level of the cost is. We know that students do borrow, sometimes extensively, to cover the cost of what is often a worthwhile investment. But students may be reluctant to take on a large amount of debt. Alternatively, they may work more while in school to reduce their debt, threatening their academic success. And from a social perspective, placing heavy debt burdens on lower-income students following graduation lessens the extent of social mobility that higher education can help achieve. For these reasons, it is desirable for college prices to be affordable to all students, and especially those from lower-income families, in the first place.

What does it mean for college to be affordable? Measuring affordability is a difficult concept. How much can a student afford? Answering that question is a key element of our financial aid system. Of course, any numeric calculation of that amount is subject to criticism, but it is impossible to calculate financial need without estimating how much a student can afford. I will review that process here. I also simulate the results of that process for families with varying financial characteristics and compare them to the net prices that different types of higher-education institutions charge them. The difference between the two provides a measure of affordability. This analysis documents important constraints facing lower-income students in our current financial aid system.

If net prices are unaffordable at four-year residential institutions for lower-income students, it would seem obvious to begin a discussion regarding ways to lower them. But will that accomplish the goal? If we lower the price that lower-income students pay, will they be more likely to attend? For those who would have chosen to attend a lower-cost institution (like a community college) otherwise, will making college more affordable alter their decision regarding where to attend? And would attending a different type of institution alter their subsequent economic well-being?

The answers to these questions are not obvious because the price is not the only obstacle that lower-income students face in the college-going process. I have already described these obstacles elsewhere, and I will return to them again in chapter 7. Their existence, though, potentially inhibits the benefits associated with reducing college pricing.

How students respond to changes in college pricing and the impact of these responses to such changes are empirical questions that have been addressed by previous research. I will also review that evidence in this chapter. In the end, there is ample reason to support a pricing system that provides a higher education at affordable prices to all families.

How Much Can Students Afford?

The Concept of "Affordability"

The term "affordability" is frequently used in discussions of college pricing. We probably can all agree that college should be affordable, but the concept is not precise. It is clearly related to its expense, but there is a difference between inexpensive and not too expensive. What does it mean for college to be affordable?

To inform a discussion of this issue, we first need to address where the money is supposed to come from to pay a student's bill. For dependent students, it seems reasonable to anticipate that the parents should be contributing to their children's educational expenditures. Very few eighteen-year-old students have sufficient resources to pay much of the cost; college represents the last expected expenditure in the parenting process, assuming the parents have the ability to pay. Some students also have grandparents who can afford to contribute to their grandchildren's education. Those children have an advantage in paying for college, but we typically do not count the grandparents' resources in thinking about ability to pay.

Perhaps a more difficult issue is what source of funds parents are supposed to use for this purpose. Current income is certainly fair game; parents who earn more should pay more.

It is when we go beyond current income that controversy arises. As an economist, I hold that the general principle should be based on command over financial resources, regardless of their source. Families with greater financial resources should pay more than families with fewer. "Resources," however, is a very broad term, and defining it in practice generates considerable ambiguity. Here, I highlight some of these issues, but it is not my intention to provide definitive answers to them.

Let us first consider the role of savings, focusing on standard asset holdings like cash in the bank, ownership of stocks and bonds (not in a retirement fund), or ownership of a tax-preferred college savings account (i.e., a "529" account). It certainly feels appropriate that these assets should "count" and that families with greater holdings should pay more to send their children to college.

This is not without controversy, though. Consider two families with annual incomes of $75,000 (roughly the median income for families with children approaching college age) each year since their children were born. One family has lived frugally, religiously saving what they could for their child's college education, while the other spent more and saved nothing. At the time their children are ready to attend college, the first family will have command over greater resources at that time. They will receive less financial aid, and they will be expected to pay more for college. Does that provide a disincentive for them to save?

And what about retirement savings or home equity? Families with greater values of these assets have command over greater resources. Again, consider two families with $75,000 in annual income, where one has $250,000 in a retirement account and $100,000 in home equity, while the other has neither. Can they afford to pay the same amount to send their children to college? The first family needs those retirement funds later in life to retire, and they need a place to live, so perhaps those funds should not count. On the other hand, the second family still has to pay rent and will also need money for retirement, so their current income needs to incorporate the use of those funds as well.

Then there is the issue of borrowing. From an economic perspective, the greater lifetime income that a college graduate will receive is a resource. Why should we not expect that student to pay for some of their education with the proceeds of that investment by taking out a loan? However, if risk-averse students avoid attending college because of those loans or if imperfections in the student loan market make it difficult for students to borrow "enough," then this limits the value of relying on using debt to pay for college.

And how do we treat families that have more than one child? Families with multiple children face higher living expenses, and paying for their children to attend college will be more of a burden. If they are in college at the same time, the stress on current income would be even greater and perhaps a larger discount may be necessary. Two otherwise identical families who space their births differently, however, face the same lifetime costs of raising their children. Is it fair for those whose children are born farther apart to pay more for college?

Even when we put aside these complicated issues of what should count as a financial resource and focus just on current income, there are still difficult issues involved in determining what "affordable" means. Let us return to the student from a family with an annual income of $75,000. How much could they afford to pay to send their child to college? Certainly not sticker price, even at a public institution. This family obviously has legitimate expenses beyond paying for college that it needs to pay (housing, food, utilities, insurance, etc.). For most families in this situation, there is not a lot of (or any?) money left over at the end of the month. And this is not a low-income family.

How much could this family spend on college costs? Probably not a lot. Is a $5,000 out-of-pocket cost affordable? That depends on what your definition of affordable is. It may be feasible, but it would be demanding on the family. It would be easier for them if the cost was lower. Again, does affordable mean inexpensive or not too expensive?

Although this is a distinction that is obviously open to interpretation, my view is that college should be considered affordable so long as the expense is feasible. Could a family plausibly be expected to pay that amount to send their child to college? College is an investment that typically has a large payoff; it needs to be subsidized for lower- and moderate-income families to make it feasible for their children to take advantage of it. This may be a dollar amount that is more than what people want to spend, but I also think a college expense that is feasible can be justified (recall the discussion in chapter 2 regarding public goods and externalities). This view is likely shared by the colleges and universities that provide financial aid.

The Measurement of Affordability

In practice, though, those broader conceptual issues are just the starting point of the problems encountered in determining how much a family can afford. It is reasonable to expect larger payments from families with higher incomes and assets, but how do we measure them? If you are an employee of a business working 40 hours per week, perhaps with a spouse in the same situation, and that is the sole source of your family's sustenance, this is not-complicated. Your W-2 from your employer(s) identifies your income. You are likely to have a checking/savings account at a bank, maybe you own a house (relevant for institutional methodology [IM]—the formula built into the CSS Profile), and perhaps you have purchased some stocks and bonds. If that describes your finances, then collecting and reporting all this information is not that difficult and what you report can be used to help calculate how much you can afford. These circumstances likely are relevant for much of the population.

For some, though, identifying the resources that can be used to pay for college is a much more difficult task. Consider small business owners who own, say, small manufacturing facilities. The businesses have revenues and costs that, hopefully, generate profits. The business owners' income is whatever they choose to withdraw from those profits. Alternatively, those funds could be used to reinvest in the businesses. Suppose the business owners decide to make large investments in renovating their facilities right at the time when their children are heading to college. Their finances really have not changed, but their incomes now appear to be low, and they may even become eligible for considerable financial aid, despite potentially possessing significant financial resources. The financial issues associated with the owners of small businesses are a major difficulty in determining what a family can afford.

Even if we had a perfect measure of financial resources, there is still the issue of how much of those resources one could reasonably expect a family to use to pay for a child's college expenses. That requires knowing something about "reasonable" spending patterns. The purpose of the financial aid system is not to subsidize a family living beyond its means, but it does intend to account for normal living expenses. How much should the system allow for those expenses? Having a larger family definitely costs more, but how much more is a reasonable amount? Making some assumptions about food and clothing is not that complicated, but there are complexities. Some areas of the country cost a lot more to live in than others (housing, taxes, etc.). Some families experience medical issues that require what could be extensive and necessary spending. Other families face other issues that make it difficult to capture expenditures (the costs of caring for a child with special needs, for instance).

If all of that were not complicated enough, then there is the issue of family structure. If a student lives with their two biological or adoptive parents, then it is straightforward to determine who we should consider responsible for paying the tuition bill. What about different family structures, though?

Take the example of separated or divorced parents. Should we only expect payment from the "custodial" parent (i.e., the one the student primarily lives with)? What if divorced parents remarry? Their finances are likely integrated at least to some extent with those of the stepparents. How do we separate those resources and determine affordability now? In the end, figuring out how much money a family has available to spend on college for their child is not a simple task.

The decisions made that address all these conceptual and practical issues are incorporated into the federal methodology (FM), which uses the FAFSA, and the institutional methodology (IM), which uses the CSS Profile. Particularly with the CSS Profile, institutions also have some flexibility in setting some of the parameters used in the formula (like the treatment of home equity). Details regarding the IM approach are available in Collins (2016), and the College Board (2014) provides an overview of the differences between IM and FM, which I also highlighted in chapter 1.

None of this is straightforward, and all of it contributes to the complexity of the financial aid system. The entire purpose of that system is designed to figure out how much one can afford to pay. Comparing that to an institution's cost of attendance (COA) determines one's "financial need." Overall, neither system is completely satisfying, but the issues are sufficiently complicated that no set of decisions and assumptions could conceivably address all possible issues.

The estimates that result from the FAFSA and CSS Profile process are labeled the expected family contribution (EFC), which is intended to measure how much a family can afford. In reality, the EFC is really just an educated guess of what a student can truly afford. With no better alternative, though, I will rely on it for the remainder of this discussion; one should keep in mind the important limitations involved in doing so.

Estimates of How Much Students Can Afford

If we are going to determine how much students can afford based on their calculated EFC, we need to apply the formulas embedded in the institutional and/or federal methodologies to data on the detailed financial characteristics of students approaching college age. The data requirements to do so, however, are daunting (not to mention the fact that the IM formula is proprietary) and far beyond anything in a publicly available database.

It is possible, though, to estimate EFC using much more limited information. I apply an algorithm designed to approximate the way institutions

use family finances to estimate it based on the work that I do with MyinTuition Corp. As I discussed in the introduction, MyinTuition is an online tool
that dozens of colleges and universities use to provide ballpark financial
aid estimates based on a small number of financial inputs and the number
of siblings enrolled in college. Minor differences across schools exist in the
computation of EFC, but the approach I use would be relevant for typical
institutions. It also blends the use of IM and FM. To simplify the subsequent analysis and discussion, I restrict all calculations to cases where the
family has only one child in college at a time.

I apply these algorithms to individual-level data from the 2016 Survey
of Consumer Finances (SCF, described in chapter 3), forecasting EFC for
all families with children between the ages of thirteen and seventeen. Figure 5.1 presents the results of this analysis. I report the percentage of students that fit within specific EFC bands. These bands can be used to gauge
several dimensions of college affordability (all at four-year, residential institutions), including

1. students with an EFC below $6,000 are Pell eligible;
2. students with an EFC below $30,000 generally are eligible for financial aid at all
   institutions;

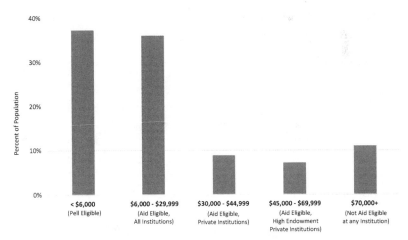

FIGURE 5.1. Distribution of expected family contribution, families with children between the
ages of thirteen and seventeen

Source: Author's calculations based on data from the 2016 Survey of Consumer Finances.

3. students with an EFC below $45,000 generally are eligible for financial aid at all private colleges;
4. students with an EFC below $70,000 generally are eligible for financial aid at private colleges with a large endowment;
5. students with an EFC above $70,000 generally are not eligible for financial aid at an institution.

The results indicate that 37 percent of students approaching college age would be Pell eligible. The data reported in table 1.4 indicate that students at flagship/R1 public institutions and private four-year large-endowment institutions enroll a much lower percentage of Pell-eligible students— 25 percent and 17 percent, respectively. Other four-year public institutions and private institutions with smaller endowments enroll 43 percent and 38 percent, respectively, which is a roughly representative share of students in this lower-income category.

Only a minority of potential students can afford to pay the full COA at any category of four-year institution. Roughly one-quarter can afford that amount at public institutions, 18 percent at private institutions with smaller endowments, and 11 percent of students at private institutions with larger endowments. The financial aid system plays a critical role in enabling students to enroll at these institutions.

What Students Can Afford Relative to What They Are Asked to Pay

Since most individuals cannot afford to pay the full sticker price at four-year institutions, how well does the financial aid system do in filling the gap between what students can afford and the financial aid that they would receive? This calculation requires information on individual net price, not average net price. As examples, I select the same percentiles of the income and asset distribution that I described earlier, with the financial characteristics listed in table 3.2. I already described an exercise reporting individual net prices for students with those characteristics at the different categories of institutions, reported in table 3.3 and figure 3.2.

The next step in comparing individual net prices to how much students can afford is to calculate EFCs for those sample students. The preceding exercise using SCF data described an approach for estimating those values, relying on an algorithm designed to translate income and assets into EFCs. I used that same approach here. Table 5.1 reports values of EFC

TABLE 5.1. How much families can "afford" to pay

Income/Assets	Expected Family Contribution (EFC)	"Affordable Net Price"
10th Percentile	$0	$8,000
25th Percentile	$600	$8,600
50th Percentile	$11,700	$19,700
75th Percentile	$31,300	$39,300
90th Percentile	$83,100	$91,100

Source: Author's calculations based on an algorithm designed to closely match the way institutions estimate EFCs applied to income and asset data obtained from the 2016 Survey of Consumer Finances. The "affordable net price" is defined as: EFC + $5,500 (Federal Student Loan) + $2,500 (work-study).

for students at the 10th, 25th, 50th, 75th, and 90th percentiles of the income and asset distributions (which do not change by type of institution).

Not surprisingly, EFC rises with family financial resources. Note that the student whose family is at the 10th percentile of the income and asset distributions cannot afford to pay anything. At the 25th percentile of these distributions, the family can afford to pay $600, according to these calculations. That means that any family in the bottom quartile of the income/asset distribution would require financial assistance to cover virtually the entire cost of a college degree. Families with incomes/assets at the 90th percentile or higher are unlikely to be eligible for financial aid based on need at any institution (at least those with only one child in college).

The EFC is designed to measure how much a family would be able to afford to pay to a higher-educational institution. Most schools, though, expect additional payments from students. This may come in the form of a federal student loan, which may be as high as $5,500 in a student's first year in college if both the subsidized and unsubsidized part of the federal student loan are taken out. Some schools expect less than this (and a handful do not expect that the student will take out any loans), but I incorporate this higher value to capture an upper bound on what a student could realistically afford to pay.

In addition, it is not unreasonable to expect students to work a modest amount during the semester to contribute toward their costs. This is the essence of the work-study program. A common value of these student earnings is $2,500. A student can earn that amount on a job that lasts thirty weeks at seven hours per week at twelve dollars an hour. This is a workload that does not seem overwhelming for students and enables them to contribute to the cost of their education. This funding could come directly from the work-study program or from a private-sector job; there is no financial difference from the student's perspective.

Combining the loan and the student employment, this provides an additional $8,000 in funds available to help pay for college. Again, some institutions may incorporate smaller values of "self-help" (the term used for this combined source of funds) than this in calculating financial aid packages, but this level is chosen to be reasonably expansive in terms of what students can afford.

The second column in table 5.1 simply adds the $8,000 to the EFC reported in the first column. I am defining this amount to be the "affordable net price" (EFC + $5,500 federal student loan + $2,500 student work). Different assumptions about the proper level of self-help can be incorporated easily in this framework.

An institution is deemed to be affordable to a student if the affordable net price is greater than the net price that the student is charged (recognizing that many assumptions have been incorporated into determining the affordable net price). The greater the difference, the more affordable. A negative value indicates that the institution is not affordable to the student; the amount they can afford is less than what they are charged. In summary, I construct the statistic, affordable net price minus actual net price as a measure of affordability. This approach is similar to that taken by the National College Attainment Network (Debaun and Warick, 2019).

Figure 5.2 and table 5.2 present these calculations of affordability for students at different percentiles of the income/asset distributions at different types of institutions (as reported in table 3.2). Data on individualized net prices are taken from table 3.3 and the affordable net price estimates come from table 5.1.

The results indicate that there are, indeed, trouble spots in the financial aid landscape. For students at the 25th percentile of the income/asset distribution or below, the net price that students are charged at public institutions is roughly $4,000 to $6,000 more than they can afford. For households with limited economic resources (incomes below $37,000 and limited assets), this would appear to be an insurmountable hurdle.

At private institutions that do not have large endowments, the gap is extensive for those in the bottom quartile. They provide financial aid that falls about $12,000 to $13,000 short of what students would need to afford that education. This is a level that would be virtually impossible for the student to make up. Lower-income students who attend these institutions would need extensive outside scholarship funding to do so. Perhaps very high-ability students would receive sufficient merit funding from the institution to cover the difference as well (my calculations already assume the

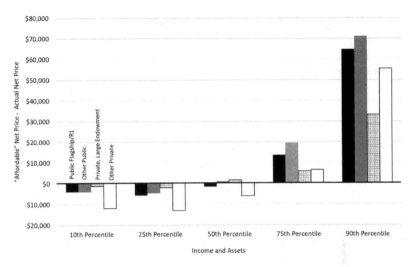

FIGURE 5.2. College affordability, by type of four-year residential institution

Source: Author's calculations.

Note: "Affordable" net price is defined as EFC + $5,500 (loan) + $2,500 (work-study), where the EFC is estimated. The actual net price is obtained from institutions' net price calculators.

TABLE 5.2. College affordability, by type of institution and level of income and assets

Income/Assets	Public Flagship/R1	Other Public	High-Endowment Private	Other Private
		Individual Net Price		
10th Percentile	$12,100	$12,000	$9,300	$19,900
25th Percentile	$14,300	$13,300	$10,700	$21,600
50th Percentile	$21,400	$18,700	$18,100	$25,800
75th Percentile	$25,700	$19,700	$33,500	$32,800
90th Percentile	$26,400	$20,000	$58,000	$35,600
		"Affordable Net Price" – Individual Net Price		
10th Percentile	-$4,100	-$4,000	-$1,300	-$11,900
25th Percentile	-$5,700	-$4,700	-$2,100	-$13,000
50th Percentile	-$1,700	$1,000	$1,600	-$6,100
75th Percentile	$13,600	$19,600	$5,800	$6,500
90th Percentile	$64,700	$71,100	$33,100	$55,500

Source: Author's calculations using data obtained from randomly selected online net price calculators from fifty institutions in each school category. See notes to table 5.1 for a discussion of "affordable net price."

student's SAT/ACT score is in the 75th percentile with a 3.67 GPA). But without some other form of support, these students are largely excluded from this category of institution.

Private institutions with large endowments do not exhibit this problem. Many schools in this category meet full need, so it is not surprising that there is virtually no gap. Institutions in this category, though, represent a small minority of colleges and are typically only an option for the highest achieving students.

Once we get to students at the 50th percentile of income and assets, most institutions are affordable, based on this definition. These students can afford to pay a net price of around $19,700 (including loans and work-study) according to these calculations, and this is about what most of these institutions charge them. A small gap still remains at public flagship/R1 institutions, but these calculations ignore the American Opportunity Tax Credit, which would reduce college costs up to an additional $2,500; middle-income families are the primary beneficiaries of this credit. Private institutions with smaller endowments still struggle to make themselves financially attractive to these students. The shortfall now is around $5,000.

At the 75th percentile, all categories of institutions are affordable. In fact, students attending public institutions are getting a good deal at these institutions. They can afford considerably more than they are charged. This result is more pronounced for students at the 90th percentile of the income/asset distribution.

As I discussed in chapter 2, ability to pay and willingness to pay are related, if not identical, concepts. When there is a gap between willingness to pay and what one must pay, we call that "consumer surplus." These statistics suggest that students from higher-income families are receiving considerable consumer surplus at most institutions.

These data also provide further justification for the influential findings of Sara Goldrick-Rab's work on the financial difficulties that lower-income college students face (Goldrick-Rab, 2016). It is not surprising that they face these difficulties when the costs they have to pay to attend college are considerably beyond what they can afford. This shows up in the numbers as well as in the students' lives. Goldrick-Rab argues that the EFC numbers that I am using here understate the true cost of living that college students face. If so, college is even more unaffordable for lower-income students than my analysis suggests. Regardless, these two approaches at assessing affordability are complementary and generate the same basic conclusion.

The notion that college is affordable for those in the middle class, at least at public and highly endowed private institutions, may seem counterintuitive to many. There are several potential explanations for this apparent contradiction. First, part of the issue may be related to families' focus on sticker price and not the actual net price paid, as detailed in chapter 4. These families cannot afford the sticker price. Second, this analysis defines "affordable" as "feasible"; it still would not be easy for families to pay that price, which may make it feel unaffordable to them. Third, families may try to pay for college from current income only, which makes the cost seem excessive at that time, but saving and borrowing are appropriate tools to pay for college as well. Finally, it is possible that the way affordability is determined in the FM and IM systems overstates the amount these families really can afford to pay. With no other alternative, I rely exclusively on those systems to determine affordability.

Would Lowering the Actual Price Increase Enrollment?

So far, I have provided evidence indicating that most schools charge students from lower-income families more than they can afford. Clearly, that is a barrier. It seems reasonable that reducing or removing that barrier would increase enrollment. As every Econ 101 student knows, when a good becomes cheaper, people purchase more of it; demand curves slope downward. But this conclusion ignores the fact that students from lower-income families face barriers to college entry that go beyond just pricing. Lowering the price for them may not increase enrollment because these other barriers still exist. The impact of reducing the price is a question that requires evidence to thoroughly address.

This question is one that has received considerable research attention. Outstanding reviews of that work can be found in Deming and Dynarski (2010), Dynarski and Scott-Clayton (2013), Page and Scott-Clayton (2016), and Nguyen, Kramer, and Evans (2019). My goal here is to provide some of the highlights from this research, focusing on more recent analyses, referring the reader seeking greater detail to those sources.

The interventions tested include three broad types of policies. First, there are aid programs that are exclusively need based, like the Pell Grant; if your income is low enough, you receive the aid. Second, there are merit-based policies; if you do well enough in high school, you receive a grant. The Hope Scholarship in Georgia and Tennessee reflect this type of program. Third, there are hybrid programs that provide aid to financially needy students who have had considerable academic success in high school. Based on the focus of this book, I will concentrate this discussion on the need-based programs (with or without an academic merit component).

Policies differ in scope beyond need versus merit. Some are targeted at high school students with an emphasis on college enrollment (sometimes specifically at four-year institutions); others focus on persistence (continuing through college) and graduation among currently enrolled college students. Some provide financial assistance only, whereas others provide additional support services as well.

Methods differ as well. A few introduce randomized controlled trials (RCTs), which I described previously in chapter 4. These exercises have the potential of providing clear and convincing evidence of a causal effect, if one is observed, at the expense of greater costs, longer durations to collect and analyze the data, and perhaps some ethical concerns regarding providing a meaningful benefit to one group but not another.

Since we do not have RCTs available to test everything we are interested in, we adopt other methods attempting to replicate the feel of an RCT. These methods do so in the sense that there is a group of individuals who received a treatment (pseudotreatment group) and another that did not (pseudocontrol group). No formal random assignment took place, but in a well-designed study of this type, one needs to be able to claim the two groups are essentially identical except for the treatment.

One recent study (Hendren and Sprung-Keyser, 2020), evaluated many different types of public interventions, ranging from social insurance (health, unemployment, and disability insurance), education and job training, taxes and cash transfers, and in-kind transfers. They conclude from this analysis that "there is a large 'bang for the buck' associated with a range of expenditures on children from early education to child health insurance to college expenditures" (1276). This assessment of "college expenditures" incorporates many of the different types of interventions described here and in the preceding chapter (including the Michigan Hail Scholarship).

In terms of specific interventions relevant for a discussion on college pricing, there are important lessons we can learn. One clear conclusion is also related to the pricing transparency discussion in chapter 4; the effectiveness of providing greater grant aid in the form of larger Pell Grants on initial college enrollment is limited because of the complicated nature of the system. If students cannot figure out the price today at a lower benefit level, how are they supposed to figure out the price tomorrow at a higher benefit level?

Interventions that make the current system more generous stumble on this point in the context of enrolling new students. Deming and Dynarski (2010) make a similar argument regarding changes in Pell Grants. They conclude that "highly-targeted programs such as the Pell focus their dollars on poorer students, but impose substantial paperwork burdens in order to identify the neediest. If targeted students are deterred by administrative hurdles, these programs will not work as well as intended" (298).

On the other hand, for students who are already enrolled, increasing the extent of aid—or lowering the price—increases persistence and graduation rates. That makes sense even within the current complicated system of financial aid. For those who already enrolled in the first place, they figured out the system. They still face financial barriers, though. Once they are enrolled in an institution and live with costs that are greater than their financial resources, the difficulties of remaining enrolled become real to them. It may hinder their academic progress. If policy can alleviate at least some of that economic hardship, maybe they can stay enrolled. These students have the ability to respond to the modified incentives that lower prices provide.

Sometimes these obstacles are not just financial. Students from lower-income families and/or first-generation college students may not have the personal backgrounds to draw from to be successful in college. They may have difficulty figuring out what classes to take, what to study, how to navigate the academic environment, and other problems. Difficulty overcoming these stumbling blocks may prevent financial incentives from accomplishing their goals. A comprehensive approach may be more successful.

The recent studies that I highlight here touch on all these issues. Angrist et al. (2014, 2016) and Angrist et al. (2020) describe one of the true experiments (RCTs) in this group. These researchers evaluate a scholarship program run by the Susan Thomas Buffett Foundation for residents of Nebraska. Selected recipients are chosen based on financial need and academic ability. The largest awards are worth up to $60,000 over five years for recipients who attend mainly public institutions in Nebraska. In the experiment, two thousand scholarships were awarded via random assignment. Those members of the treatment group were significantly more likely to enroll in college, attend a four-year institution, and persist relative to members of the control group. Nonwhite students and first-generation students were among the groups with the largest effects.

Two studies that are based on variability in aid awards through the Pell Grant support my earlier statement that we should likely expect those types of policy changes to affect persistence and graduation, not enrollment. Bettinger et al. (2019) use a "regression-discontinuity" design to compare students just above and below cutoff thresholds for eligibility for CalGrants (an add-on to the Pell Grant in California that works similarly, except it also includes a GPA cutoff). Those just barely eligible who received the award had greater rates of persistence and graduation relative to those who fell just short of eligibility. They did not observe any impact on enrollment. Denning, Marx, and Turner (2019) use a similar research design but focus on students in Texas who just meet the condition necessary for an "automatic zero EFC" (i.e., if their incomes are below some threshold, the student automatically receives a maximum Pell Grant), relative to those students whose incomes just miss the cutoff. Students in Texas who qualify for automatic zero EFC also receive supplemental state funding. The results from this analysis also find higher rates of persistence and graduation but no impact on enrollment at four-year colleges.

One similar study by Castleman and Long (2016) was able to find broader impacts from a program providing additional funding through the traditional financial aid system. These authors evaluate the Florida Student Access Grant, which provides additional financial aid for students with EFCs below a specific threshold. Students with EFCs just above that threshold got nothing. The results of this analysis show that grant recipients were more likely to enroll at, persist at, and graduate from a four-year university.

Two other studies examined programs that focused more specifically on persistence and graduation. One program was the Wisconsin Scholars Grant, which offered low-income students $3,500 if they remained enrolled. Goldrick-Rab et al. (2016) evaluated the grant using a true RCT to determine the program's impact. A second, the Dell Scholars program, provided financial support as well as other "life" support services to low-income students who demonstrate "grit, potential, and ambition." Page et al. (2019) compare outcomes from those who just qualified for the program to those who just missed the cutoff. Only those who were already planning to enroll in a four-year institution were considered, so it was unlikely to have much of an impact on enrollment. Both interventions demonstrated positive effects on persistence and graduation.

Would Lowering the Actual Price Affect the Type of Institution Selected?

Students can respond to lower prices by increasing their likelihood of enrollment in college at all or by enrolling at different types of institutions.

One might expect that students are well served when they attend a more selective institution that is the best fit for them. College pricing and issues of affordability may break that relationship.

For instance, community colleges provide an outstanding opportunity to enroll in college for students on the margin of attending college at all. Their relatively low cost is an important draw, and they have a proven track record of improving labor market outcomes for students who attend (Marcotte, 2019). But students who are able to enroll in four-year colleges may further improve their long-term financial well-being if they can afford it. This section will review the evidence on the impact of college pricing on the types of institutions that students attend and the impact on their subsequent earnings.

Cohodes and Goodman (2014) provide strong evidence that affordability alters enrollment patterns even among those who attend college anyway. They examine the impact of the "Adams Scholarship" in the state of Massachusetts, which subsidizes enrollment at public four-year universities for students with high test scores. The authors compared college outcomes for those just above and below the specific test-score threshold and found that recipients were more likely to attend these institutions. They found that students enrolled at these institutions at a higher rate. They also found, though, that these students would have otherwise attended institutions that were more highly ranked, with higher performing students on standardized exams, higher spending, and higher graduation rates. In the end, the award decreased the likelihood that recipients would graduate from college in four or even six years.

This study shows that differences in affordability do affect choice of institution in ways that can alter subsequent outcomes. It also shows that affordable pricing for lower-income students needs to occur at all levels of institutions. Students achieve the most when they are best matched with the selectivity of the institution they attend. Narrowing their choices creates an inefficiency that may not be beneficial to them.

Evidence also indicates that free community college programs have the power to increase enrollments of students who otherwise might not have attended college, but they also attract students who would have attended four-year institutions as well. Gurantz (2019) examines the impact of the Oregon Promise program, which initially guaranteed free community college to all state residents (higher-income students are no longer eligible). Carruthers, Fox, and Jepsen (2020) report the impact of a similar program offered to all high school seniors in Knox County, Tennessee (a precursor to the Tennessee Promise program). Both analyses compare enrollment patterns for students in those locations with those of students in comparison locations. Both find that the programs increased enrollments at community colleges, including for lower-achieving students who would not have otherwise attended college. They also offer evidence, though, that some students enrolled in a community college rather than a four-year institution.

Collectively, these results suggest that some students who would attend college anyway gravitate toward those that they find to be more affordable even if they are not the best fit for them academically. Evidence also shows that students who attend more selective schools earn higher wages later in life. The Cohodes and Goodman (2014) study does not examine earnings directly, but its finding that students from Massachusetts were less likely to graduate from college suggests that their subsequent earnings will be lower. Black, Denning, and Rothstein (2020) and Bleemer (2020) examine the impact of "top percent rules," in which more selective four-year public institutions guarantee admission to students in the top percentiles of their high school graduation cohorts. These analyses show that such policies increase enrollment at these institutions and subsequent earnings of those who benefit from the policies.

Another category of studies examines differences in student outcomes for those just above and below admissions thresholds at more selective four-year public universities based on test scores (Zimmerman, 2014; Smith, Goodman, and Hurwitz, 2020). These students can be thought of as academically similar, but those above the cutoff are more likely to attend the selective institution, whereas those just below tend to enroll in a community college. Earnings after graduation are higher for those who attend the selective institutions.

Connecting the dots, this discussion indicates that students respond to prices in terms of the type of institutions they attend. If four-year colleges are not affordable to lower-income students, that would lead them to attend less selective institutions. The evidence also indicates that doing so will reduce their subsequent earnings. Affordability affects selectivity, and selectivity matters.

Discussion

The main purpose of this chapter was to address the question of whether college is affordable and for whom. I document that financial aid does not sufficiently cover the financial needs of students at least in the bottom 25 percent of the distribution of financial resources at most institutions. Only private institutions with large endowments provide adequate financial aid to those students; these represent a small minority of colleges and universities. These students cannot afford to attend public institutions, even after incorporating generous allowances for loans and student employment. They face a gap of around $4,000 to $6,000 between what students can afford and what these institutions expect them to pay out of pocket. Some of them get around this barrier by getting help from extended family or receiving outside scholarships. Others borrow or work more, which may hinder their academic success and subsequent economic well-being. Still others are prevented from attending a four-year college, leaving community colleges as their only viable option. Private colleges with smaller endowments struggle to meet the financial needs of these students.

We also know that providing greater financial support to these students will improve their academic and subsequent labor market outcomes. This has been shown in a large body of research evidence. It will increase the likelihood that lower-income students will attend college. It will also increase the likelihood that those students attend more selective institutions, including the four-year residential colleges like the ones I focus on in this book. Both higher enrollment overall and enrollment at more selective institutions will lead to increased wages.

There are definitely some caveats that are needed after drawing this conclusion. First, if we just offer more money through a system that is already too complicated to use, it will be less effective. Simplicity and transparency in the financial aid system, which I focused on in chapter 4, is essential if we are going to get the greatest return from spending more money on financial aid. Second, the impact of reducing the cost may be enhanced if it comes along with other programs that make it easier for students to navigate the college search process in the first place. It also helps if those additional funds are supplemented with more support services provided to those students once they get there. I will address these additional constraints in chapter 7.

CHAPTER SIX

Fixing the Pricing System in Higher Education

Policy makers and higher-education institutions must find ways to lower the price paid by lower-income students to attend college. As I explained in chapter 5, college really is unaffordable for them at most institutions. The problem is that lowering actual prices reduces college revenue. To maintain spending on academic services that institutions provide, institutions would need greater revenue from other sources to replace the revenue lost by lowering the price for lower-income students.

Changing the pricing system, though, cannot work if nobody knows what those prices really are. Chapter 4 documented the problems associated with misinformation about college costs and financial aid. Does it matter if low-income students face a net price of $8,000 or $13,000 (including the maximum federal student loan and work-study) if they think it will cost them $70,000, or even $30,000? Convincing them that the sticker price does not apply to them gets us part of the way there. Charging the students what they can afford does the rest. Both elements of reform are needed.

In this chapter, I will provide greater details regarding these arguments, recap how we got into this hole, and suggest ways that we can get out of it. Initially, I will address ways to modify the pricing system within its current framework, focusing on doubling the size of the Pell Grant. Issues of pricing transparency are also clearly relevant here, and I will discuss ways to accomplish that goal within the current pricing system. After that, I will explore policy proposals for "free college," which would fundamentally transform the way that students pay for college.

Addressing the Pricing System

A Review of the Problem

We know from the analysis I presented in chapter 5 that public flagship and other four-year public universities charge lower-income students more than they can afford to pay. This leads them to be more likely to enroll in less selective institutions or not to enroll at all. The issue is more extreme at private institutions that do not have large endowments. These statistics are unlikely to be a surprise to administrators at these institutions, and they would like nothing more than to have the resources to be able to fix it.

The problem is that the money needs to come from somewhere. Enrolling lower-income students at lower net prices means a loss of revenue for higher-educational institutions. Simply reducing costs to match those lost revenues is certainly a possibility, but it is easier said than done. These institutions do not charge lower-income students less because they cannot afford to do so.

My discussion in chapter 2 describes the market mechanisms that led to this outcome. The role of (legal) price discrimination based on market power is at the heart of that discussion. Private institutions with large endowments have enough market power to price discriminate extensively, enabling them to charge more to students with greater financial resources and willingness to pay. Along with the ability to draw from their large endowments, the higher prices these institutions charge wealthier students provide the additional revenue they need to charge lower-income students less.

However, this is not possible at all other types of institutions. Presumably, many public flagship/R1 institutions have the market power to follow a similar model to this, but tuition at these institutions is capped at much lower levels and set by the state. Ironically, those caps are imposed to maintain affordability. It accomplishes that goal for middle-income students, but higher-income students end up as the biggest beneficiaries. Direct spending on higher education from the state could be used to provide greater resources to the institutions so that they could lower the price further for lower-income students. This would make them affordable for these students as well, but that tends not to happen, as documented in chapter 1. The higher spending from the state is typically used to maintain lower sticker prices, not applied to greater financial aid.

Once we move into the broader market of other public and private four-year institutions, there are so many similar institutions that they have limited market power. The greater level of competition for students among these institutions prevents them from charging substantially higher prices to students from higher-income families.

As discussed in chapter 2, the statutory caps on tuition at the public institutions exacerbate this problem in the public sector, and this spills over into the private sector. It is hard for these private institutions to charge much more than those capped prices at public institutions. They set high sticker prices but then use merit aid offered to the vast majority of their students to offset them, lowering the effective maximum price. This practice accomplishes a marketing goal, but in the end, the market plays a meaningful role in determining the maximum price that these institutions can charge. They are at a further competitive disadvantage relative to the public institutions with which they compete because they have no state funding or meaningful endowment funds. Overall, they do not have the resources to charge affordable net prices to lower-income students.

Taken as a whole, these structural constraints prevent all but a limited number of institutions from charging affordable prices to lower-income students. Private institutions without a large endowment are particularly constrained in doing so. Pricing policies throughout higher education are dictated by these market forces. They are not voluntary.

The question then becomes how do we alter this market landscape to alleviate the problem? In this discussion, I will present different approaches, but the bottom line is that they all revert to the same basic solution—higher-income individuals, whether students or taxpayers, need to pay more so that lower-income students can pay less.

Doubling the Pell Grant

One solution to the problem is to significantly expand the size of the maximum Pell Grant award for which students are eligible. It currently stands at $6,345 per year per student in 2020–21. According to my calculations reported in chapter 5 regarding what lower-income students can afford, it is at least $4,000 too low. Raising it by, say, $5,000 would significantly fill the gap in affordability for qualifying students.

In fact, doubling the size of the Pell Grant makes more sense. There are reasons to believe that the $5,000 increase (not quite double) really is not enough. This is consistent with Goldrick-Rab's (2016) finding that what it actually costs students to attend college, including all expenses, is greater than the amount the financial aid system budgets for them. It could also slightly reduce the $5,500 student loan burden that my simulation incorporates. Finally, simplicity in policy making matters, and doubling the grant satisfies that.

Mechanically, doubling the size of the maximum Pell award would also increase the share of students eligible for it. Currently, students with incomes up to perhaps $50,000 and assets typical of that income level are eligible for some level of Pell Grant. Doubling it would increase this threshold to perhaps $70,000. Around half the college-age population would be eligible for some level of Pell Grant.

Since the resources necessary to support such an increase would come from tax revenue, in a progressive system of taxation that money would come from higher-income individuals in the broader population (not just the population of families with children in college).

There are potential downsides to that proposal, though. Institutions could introduce policies that counteract the increase in federal grant aid. They could charge more (the "Bennett Hypothesis"; Bennett, 1987) or cut institutional financial aid, leaving students no better off with the same net price. That would enable colleges and universities to improve their own finances, not the students' finances, at the expense of the government.

Archibald and Feldman (2016) review the evidence regarding these potential responses. They find that "most studies conclude that . . . the amount of the federal support that winds up diverted, or taxed, by nonprofit colleges and universities seems quite low" (19), but it is still a possibility. Another review by Heller (2013) concludes "research on the relationship between federal financial aid and tuition price increases can be described as ambiguous at best" (2). In a recent analysis, Turner (2020) finds that almost 90 percent of Pell Grant funding results in additional aid provided to students.

At least at public institutions, a potential approach that could guarantee no such diversion of funds takes place is to mandate that institutions meet the full financial need of state residents in exchange for these enhanced Pell Grants. My calculations suggest that this is a feasible solution. If lower-income students at public institutions are currently receiving aid that is $4,000–$6,000 short of meeting full need, and the Pell Grant provided an additional $6,345 in grant funding, then the gap would close. With no way to divert the additional federal funds, these institutions would be unable to follow the path anticipated by the Bennett

Hypothesis. Mandating that these institutions meet full need would also satisfy reasonable equity goals.

Mandating that public institutions meet full need has a possible drawback. Institutions seeking greater revenue could meet full financial need for the students that they accept, but it could reject those with strong credentials but significant financial need. Hill (2019) highlights the trade-offs between how much a student pays and whether that student is accepted. Increasing the value of the Pell Grant, though, to a level that would enable these public institutions to meet full need should not generate that response. In essence, the finances of the institutions would remain unaffected if the gap in need is filled in with a larger Pell Grant and they were required to meet full need.

This approach is not feasible at private institutions with smaller endowments, however, because the enhanced Pell Grant would not fill the gap between what these institutions charge lower-income students and what they can afford. This gap is in the vicinity of $12,000 at these institutions, which is considerably greater than the proposed increase in Pell funding. They still would not be able to meet full need with these funds; all the other market pressures described earlier would prevent them from finding the additional necessary funding elsewhere.

Even without this provision, the recent introduction of net price calculators also provides protection against institutions' syphoning off these funds. Tracking the results from these tools can help determine whether colleges and universities manipulated their pricing in response to an increase in the Pell Grant. The estimated net price for a student with extremely limited financial resources should fall by the amount of the Pell Grant increase. If it does not, the institution is violating the intent of the policy.

Another potential downside to increasing the value of the Pell Grant is one that I have addressed previously; increasing its value does not help if people cannot navigate the system because of its complexity. Finding ways to better communicate college pricing, including the Pell Grant, is a critical issue that needs to be addressed regardless of this grant's value. I will propose ways to help students and their parents better understand college pricing below.

Overall, I find reasons to strongly support doubling the Pell Grant. It is a feasible solution that will accomplish the goal of bringing the cost of a college education within reach for lower-income students who are now currently charged more than they can afford. This would also need to be indexed to inflation to prevent its real value from eroding over time. Later in the chapter, I will compare this policy alternative to various free college proposals.

Other Potential Solutions

There are other approaches to improve access that may make sense from the perspective of the college pricing economic model that I presented in chapter 2, but they would have tremendous difficulty surviving the political process. While they are not likely feasible proposals, I present them here to clarify the underlying issues that cause the pricing problems we currently face.

One solution that could work, in principle, is an increase in state spending on higher education. In theory, that money could be used in the same way as the increase in the Pell Grant proposed earlier. What we know from past experience, though (as documented in chapter 1), is that when states choose to provide greater support for their higher-educational systems, they tend to use this money to keep the sticker price low, not to provide more need-based aid. That provides the greatest benefits to those from higher-income families and violates the premise of increasing access. Regardless of the politics of this policy, tight state budgets limit the viability of this solution.

Beyond that, the most direct solution to the affordability problem, ironically, is for public institutions to increase their sticker price. These institutions would collect more tuition revenue from higher-income students who pay the full sticker price that could be used to lower the net price for lower-income students who receive financial aid (Cook and Turner, 2021). In essence, this is a direct application of a high-tuition, high-aid model. A side benefit of this approach is that it would spill over to the private institutions with whom these public institutions compete. What higher-income students pay at these institutions is influenced by low sticker prices at public institutions. If the public institutions adopted a more progressive pricing policy, the private institutions could as well.

Yet a high-tuition, high-aid model is not popular because it often ends up supporting a high-tuition, low-aid policy. Turner (2018) summarizes much of the controversy regarding this model. Higher-income families would oppose paying more, and lower-income families are very likely to wrongly believe that they would have to pay more as well. Most people believe that higher tuition makes college more unaffordable, and so they favor restrictions on price increases, if allowed at all.

But as I have shown, in reality, a low sticker price *is* what makes college unaffordable for lower-income students. The beneficiaries of a low sticker price system are students from higher-income families. The low sticker price makes college more affordable for higher-income families and less affordable for lower-income families. Nonetheless, political realities make this approach an unlikely possibility.

Another feasible, but likely unpopular, proposal is one that is not common for an economist to endorse—support collusion across institutions. In chapter 2, I described two instances in which the US Department of Justice intervened in the higher-education market over the past thirty years, with the specific goal of increasing competition. In typical markets, greater competition is beneficial; it will generally lead to lower market prices, and that is better for consumers. Active government involvement to promote competition is generally helpful.

In this case, though, it reduces the ability for higher-education institutions to price discriminate. Institutions could agree to charge higher prices to higher-income students and lower prices to lower-income students. That is how progressive financing systems work. And doing so advances the public good. It provides economic opportunity to more individuals, a clearly desirable feature of a society and one that we could use more of in the United States.

Collusion in the system of providing merit awards is another area where it may be beneficial to relax antitrust policy. In chapter 2, I described how these awards represent a prisoner's dilemma. Once one institution offers merit awards to attract high-achieving students, all others need to follow. In the end, no one institution has a price advantage for these students; each institution ends up with the same number of them that they would have had otherwise. Since these merit awards received by lower-income students largely reduce the need-based aid those students receive, the students who mainly benefit from them are those from higher-income families. The only result from this process is that the revenue institutions received from students falls, and that provides fewer resources for institutions to offer need-based aid to lower-income students.

Allowing collusion to enforce an agreement where each institution refrained from offering these merit awards would increase college access. Again, prices would rise for higher-income students and fall for lower-income students.

It is unclear whether greater support for collusion among colleges would require legislation, whether existing laws would need to be interpreted differently, or whether the US Department of Justice simply looked the other way when colleges went ahead and acted collectively. Regardless of the method, we would benefit if collusion among higher-education institutions were allowed in support of a more progressive financial aid system. The general political sentiment, though, that competition is a good thing (which it often is) makes such an approach unlikely to be implemented.

Addressing Pricing Simplicity and Transparency

As I indicated earlier, doubling the Pell Grant to improve access only works if students understand how much they would have to pay to attend college after factoring in financial aid. It will not work if we do not do a better job communicating those prices. Students and their parents need to be able to forecast how much they are going to have to pay well in advance of the college decision, and then they need to process the necessary forms without being overburdened when they apply. Both sets of changes are necessary if we are going to resolve problems associated with college pricing.

Recent Legislative Activity

Shortcomings in our system of providing financial aid have been noted by policy makers and several legislative proposals have been introduced attempting to address different aspects of it. The National Association of Student Financial Aid Officers (NASFAA) tracks these legislative proposals at https://www.nasfaa.org/legislative_tracker and https://www.nasfaa .org/higher_education_act_reauthorization.

One noteworthy legislative victory came in very early 2021 (just as this book is being written) in the form of the Consolidated Appropriations Act. Although the primary purpose of this law is to fund much of the government for the 2021 fiscal year, it includes a subsection that calls for the simplification of FAFSA beginning in the 2023–24 academic year (which was subsequently pushed back by one year to 2024–25). The details of the law are not clear as I write this, but a description of its provisions as currently known are provided in NASFAA Policy & Federal Relations Staff (2021).

The law contains several provisions designed to make it easier for students to understand the financial aid available to them. For instance, eligibility for the maximum Pell Grant mainly will be determined based on family income. A dependent student with one sibling would be eligible for the maximum Pell Grant if the family's adjusted gross income is below $46,375 in a single parent household or $49,410 in a two-parent household.

Below the maximum grant, the benefit would be determined according to a formula similar to the one that exists today with some changes to the process. First, the law will make it easier to transfer the income information used in the calculations from the IRS, eliminating the need to answer those questions.

Second, the expected family contribution (EFC) will be relabeled the Student Aid Index (SAI). The reason for the change is that the EFC label does not adequately convey what the reported value is really expressing. In financial aid language, a "contribution" is a euphemism for a payment, so one might imagine families interpret the EFC as the expected payment. Unless an institution meets full need, however, that is not what the EFC means, and most institutions do not meet full need. Relabeling the resulting value as the SAI more clearly indicates that it is just an input into the process of determining financial aid, not the result of that process. In the new system, Pell Grant awards below the maximum will be determined as total need less SAI, much like it currently is calculated based on total need less EFC. It is just a label change.

Again, though, this step does not address the fundamental problem of communicating affordability. What do we learn from the SAI? It still does not tell you the final price that an institution is going to charge a student incorporating all forms of financial aid. That is what students need to know: *What is college going to cost me?* Since every college is different, as are their methods to distribute institutional financial aid, more information is needed than just the EFC/SAI. Net price calculators were supposed to solve that problem, but I have already documented their limitations in accomplishing that goal. Even once the SAI is known, a black box still remains in determining a final financial aid award.

There are other provisions included in this legislation that affect both the amount of a Pell Grant and how it is communicated, but the provisions I have highlighted are the most significant. In the end, there is no question that these are useful steps that help begin to make the financial aid process more transparent for students and their families, but there is still considerably more work left to be done.

Indeed, one recent proposal, the Student Aid Improvement Act (sponsored by former Senator Lamar Alexander, R-TN, who led the drive for the FAFSA simplification enacted in early 2021), includes language promoting communication of actual pricing. When students complete the FAFSA, they would receive additional information for institutions they choose regarding net prices by income category, graduation rates, loan default rates, etc. But all of this is already available on the College Scorecard. I have previously described the limitations of that source for financial aid information; those shortcomings would persist. This act, however, does not go far enough in getting students what they need: a simpler financial aid process that enables students to better understand the full amount of aid they are eligible for. Besides these limitations, it ignores the issues faced by the hundreds of institutions that also rely on the CSS Profile to determine financial aid awards. More work is needed here.

The Net Price Calculator Improvement Act, sponsored by Senator Chuck Grassley (R-IA), is another relevant, recent legislative proposal. As its name suggests, it is designed to improve net price calculators. One set of provisions is designed to standardize the information presented. Another main feature of this act is the creation of a "universal calculator" that would enable students to enter a single set of inputs and get estimates at multiple institutions. One significant limitation of that approach is that the universal calculator would need to include any question that any school included in their own net price calculator, which could balloon the number of questions asked. It is not clear to me whether that proposal would make the system simpler or more complicated.

College Pricing Transparency: What We Need

The main remaining problem is that we still need to go back further to help those students who are just starting to think about going to college. Students and their parents start forming aspirations early. They may think, perhaps incorrectly, that they cannot possibly afford college, which will certainly curb their aspirations. They need a way to gauge what college is going to cost. That is exactly the issue that the College Scorecard and net price calculators were designed to address, but as my earlier discussion clarifies, they do not adequately accomplish their goal.

In my view, what we need is a process by which students can start the college search process using the simplest possible tools to obtain a very rough, individualized, estimate of what a college is going to cost. The point of that exercise is to refocus students and their families away from the sticker price (unless they have significant financial means and the sticker price is appropriate) and consider the possibility that their cost may be (considerably?) less than that. They can then enter more information along the way and refine their estimates. Eventually, they complete a financial aid form and get an actual financial aid award.

I refer to this concept as a financial aid information funnel—start at

the top with limited information and provide individualized, ballpark estimates. These estimates may be imprecise, but at an early stage of the process it is useful for students to know whether the sticker price is appropriate
for them. It likely is not, and learning that lesson early, quickly, and easily is
important. As students advance through the process, they provide more information and get more precise estimates. Ultimately, they go through the
formal financial aid application process and receive an exact final answer.
We need to keep people moving through the process without scaring them
off. Asking a hard question at the beginning part of the process will do that.
Asking a harder question later in the process, after applicants have a sense
of what the final answer will be, is less daunting.

All of this can take place over the course of months (years?). The idea
is to let prospective students move slowly through the necessary gates to
get to the final answer rather than letting them wander aimlessly and then
throwing up a huge barricade they need to overcome right at the end.

Consider an online tool that initially only asks for family income and
number of siblings in college (similar to John Monro's 1953 system at Harvard) and returns an estimated range based on historical data from that
institution. For instance, the results could indicate that for families with an
income level of $60,000 and no siblings in college, most students can expect
to pay between $X and $Y, with a best estimate of $Z, where $X and $Y
are the upper and lower bounds from a 90 percent confidence interval (i.e.,
90 percent of students at that income level would pay within that range).
The income requested should be total income, not adjusted gross income.
Avoiding technical language from the tax system at early stages in the process is key to reducing the anxiety of prospective students/families. Even if
that range is quite large—and it will be if we just use income—it will still
give the vast majority of students real insight into how much lower their
actual cost of attending college may be compared to the sticker price.

To narrow the range, we can next ask for basic asset information. Families above the income limits established to use the "Simplified Needs Test"
(which eliminates the need for these families to enter asset information on
the FAFSA) must provide asset data to complete the FAFSA and all families who complete the CSS Profile have to provide full details regarding
their assets. At an early stage of the process, though, the system could request information on the most common, and easily known, forms of assets
(cash, home equity, stocks and bonds outside of a retirement account). The
net price forecast including that information should provide a smaller range
of estimates, if not necessarily small.

Next, students would complete the FAFSA or CSS Profile, incorporating the beneficial changes proposed and discussed earlier. The result of the process generates a value of the EFC/SAI. Then enter the EFC/SAI into an institution-specific calculator to get a net price estimate at an institution that, at that point, should be reasonably precise with a relatively narrow range. If, and when, students are admitted, they would receive a financial aid award with a well-constructed and understandable award letter (an issue addressed in detail in chapter 7), and the process is complete. Institutions could opt to include a simplified merit award estimate into the process.

One important element that this approach adds that is currently missing is the notion of a confidence interval around an estimate. Currently, no formal net price calculator includes a confidence interval; they provide single estimates. The recipient of an estimate is likely to believe that the result is closely linked to what they will pay (disclaimers are provided to the contrary, but the psychology is that the result is the result).

My conversations with financial aid professionals indicate this is a significant problem. They routinely hear from admitted students who have applied for financial aid, "Why do I have to pay so much more than the result I received from your net price calculator?" The answer, of course, is that the information used on the FAFSA or CSS Profile is more extensive than that included in the net price calculator. Providing full details may yield considerably different results. Besides, people do not always fully understand what is being asked of them. What is the difference between total income, adjusted gross income, and taxable income? As a result, they enter incorrect values. It would be much better to implement a process whereby people do not feel like they have been misled.

Free College and the Pricing System

In the current policy environment, any discussion of college pricing and affordability needs to address proposals regarding free college. The idea behind free college is to extend the free public education system beyond high school and through the level of higher education. In a modern economy with greater needs for a more skilled workforce, a college education today is more like a high school education from the past, and we should guarantee its provision for free, the thinking goes.

In chapter 2, I discussed the notion of public goods in the context of higher education. In that discussion, I highlighted that higher education does not satisfy the conditions of a public good, particularly with the high private return to a college education. It does generate considerable positive externalities, however; society benefits broadly from having a more highly educated population and workforce. Income-targeted subsidies for higher education make sense. That works against the notion of free college and in favor of policies like extended Pell Grants, as I discussed earlier in this chapter.

Given the relevance of free college to current public discussions, though, the data and methods I have introduced in this book are useful for evaluating the strengths and weaknesses of alternative specific proposals for free college. To evaluate them, I examine how students at different points in the income distribution fare if each were enacted. I conclude that free college is not the answer to the problems I have highlighted in this book.

Specific Policies

The two most important aspects of the different proposals for free college are whether they are universal (versus limited to those below some income threshold) and how the policies interact with existing forms of financial aid, including Pell Grants. The specific plans I will evaluate are based on New York State's Excelsior Scholarship, which is already in place, two of Bernie Sanders's "College for All" plans (one proposed in 2017 and another in 2019), and Joe Biden's "Plan for Education beyond High School." As a point of comparison, I will also discuss a policy of doubling the maximum Pell Grant, as I described earlier in this chapter. It is similar to a proposal in Joe Biden's higher-education policy plan during the primaries. For reference, the main features of these plans are detailed in table 6.1.

The Excelsior Scholarship was implemented in New York State in 2017. It currently provides free tuition and fees at public institutions for students coming from families earning under $125,000 per year. It does not cover living expenses like room and board, though, which are a significant component of the cost of attendance (COA). A key feature of this policy is that the benefits from this program displace true need-based aid. A Pell Grant, for instance, does not augment the subsidy provided by the free tuition and fees (described at https:/www.suny.edu/smarttrack/types -of-financial-aid/scholarships/excelsior). A student cannot receive both.

Bernie Sanders's first College for All plan was introduced as a bill in the Senate in 2017 (bill S. 806 in the 115th Congress). It proposed eliminating

TABLE 6.1. Alternative free college/college affordability plan provisions

Plan	Income Threshold	Interaction with Other Forms of Financial Aid
Double Pell (Biden 2019)	EFC = $12,690 (around $70,000 income)[*]	Doubles maximum Pell Grant
NYS Excelsior Scholarship	$125,000	Tuition remission replaces other cash grants
"College for All" (Sanders 2017)	$125,000	Other cash grants remain intact
"College for All" (Sanders 2019)	None	Other cash grants remain intact
Double Pell and 2017 College for All (Biden 2020)	$125,000	Doubles maximum Pell Grant; students can receive both

[*]Assumes asset levels at a comparable point in the asset distribution.

tuition and fees for families with incomes up to $125,000 at different types of institutions including public four-year colleges and universities, the focus of this analysis. The 2019 plan (bill S. 1947 in the 116th Congress) dropped the income limit and would have also canceled all student loan debt. Importantly, the tuition subsidy included in these bills would not displace other forms of federal aid. Students would be allowed to use Pell Grants to pay for their other expenses while in college, including room and board.

In Joe Biden's presidential campaign, he proposed incorporating the provisions of Sanders's 2017 plan along with his own earlier proposal to double the value of the Pell Grant to almost $13,000 (https://joebiden.com/beyondhs). Students would have the opportunity to benefit from both forms of aid. This proposal was also included in the 2020 Democratic Party platform. At the time this book was written, it remained too early to tell what specific policy the Biden administration will pursue (if any).

Impact on Affordability

I use the data and methodological framework described earlier in this book to address the distributional consequences of these proposals. Specifically, I evaluate the impact on cost and affordability for students/families with different levels of financial resources, defined by percentiles in the income and asset distributions. I start with the comparisons presented in chapter 5 (table 5.2) of net price paid and "affordable net price" at public flagship/R1 institutions (costs at private institutions are not directly affected, and results for other public institutions are similar). For public flagship/R1 institutions, I show in chapter 1 that the average COA (sticker price) is $27,100, and the average level of tuition and fees is $11,000, based on Integrated Postsecondary Education Data System (IPEDS) data for 2017–18. Then I simulate the impact on net prices resulting from each of these proposals.

The results of this analysis are provided in table 6.2. Doubling the Pell Grant lowers the net price for students at the 10th and 25th percentiles to $5,800 and $8,600, respectively. These values are at or below the calculated affordable net price ($8,000 and $8,600, respectively). For the lowest income category, this would partially satisfy the concerns expressed by Goldrick-Rab (2016) that lower-income students have expenses that go beyond what these universities expect. Beyond that, students at the 50th percentile receive no benefit from doubling the Pell Grant. They were paying a net price that is a little above what they can afford at state flagship/R1 institutions, but this calculation does not incorporate the American Opportunity Tax Credit, which is worth $2,500; these individuals are prime beneficiaries of this credit. Higher-income students receive no benefit, but they were also already paying prices that these calculations indicate they can afford.

Policies like the Excelsior Scholarship are evaluated in the next column. A free college policy like that one would eliminate the $11,000 average value of tuition and fees. It displaces, though, other forms of financial aid. In the end, it offers no benefit to students from lower-income families, who would have received considerable aid otherwise. That other aid is greater than the level of tuition and fees that these students would be exempt from paying under this policy, and they cannot receive both. It also offers no benefit to those at the top of the income distribution because they surpass the $125,000 income threshold, eliminating the benefit. Their net price remains unchanged. Only students from families in the 50th and 75th percentiles of the income distribution would pay less, with the largest benefit going to those at the 75th percentile (almost $120,000 in family income).

A broader range of students benefit from the College for All plans because the tuition benefit provided by this policy does not preclude receipt of other forms of aid. The only difference between the impacts of the 2017 and 2019 plans are for the students at the 90th percentile of the income and asset distributions, as shown in the next two columns of the table. Lower-income students fare very well under this system. If all other forms of financial aid continue as in the current system, students at the 10th and

TABLE 6.2. Comparison of free college to current system, public flagship/R1 universities

				Net Price under Alternative Proposals			
Income/Assets	"Affordable Net Price"	Current Net Price	Double Pell	NYS Excelsior Scholarship	College for All 2017	College for All 2019	Double Pell and College for All
10th Percentile (income = $19,900)	$8,000	$12,100	$5,800	$12,100	$1,100	$1,100	-$5,200
25th Percentile (income = $36,600)	$8,600	$14,300	$8,600	$14,300	$3,300	$3,300	-$2,400
50th Percentile (income = $70,100)	$19,700	$21,400	$21,400	$16,100	$10,400	$10,400	$10,400
75th Percentile (income = $119,300)	$39,300	$25,700	$25,700	$16,100	$14,700	$14,700	$14,700
90th Percentile (income = $210,300)	$91,100	$26,400	$26,400	$26,400	$26,400	$15,400	$26,400

Note: All calculations are rounded to the nearest $100 and are based on an average cost of attendance at public flagship/R1 institutions of $27,100 and tuition and fees of $11,000 (estimates obtained from IPEDS data for the 2017–18 academic year). College for All 2019 is the only policy that provides benefits with no income threshold.

25th percentiles of the income and asset distributions would pay $1,100 and $3,300, respectively. Middle- and upper-income students would do well under this system as well, although the $125,000 income threshold would mean that families in the 90th percentile would not be affected by the 2017 plan.

The calculations presented here regarding College for All assume that all existing forms of financial aid would remain intact, simply augmented by the removal of tuition and fees. The proposed legislation attempted to accomplish this through formal language maintaining the Pell Grant and inducements to states to maintain other forms of support for financial aid. Maintaining these other forms of aid would be essential for the success of such a policy. Otherwise, if these other forms of aid were reduced or eliminated, the benefits would only go to middle- and upper-middle-class students (50th and 75th percentiles in table 6.2) under the 2017 plan and all middle-class students and above (50th percentile and above in table 6.2) under the 2019 plan.

Moreover, the fact that Sanders's 2019 plan provides a uniform benefit throughout the income distribution skews the benefit to the rich. McFarland et al. (2019) report that 79 percent of students from families in the top quintile of the socioeconomic status (closely linked to income) distribution attend college right after high school, compared to 32 percent from the bottom quintile. Higher-income students would be more than twice as likely to receive a benefit that is of equal size per student relative to lower-income students. It is a particularly poorly targeted approach to making college affordable.

The final proposal I evaluate is the one introduced by Joe Biden, incorporating the recommendations of the "Unity Taskforce," designed to unify Biden and Bernie Sanders in opposition to Donald Trump in the 2020 election. In terms of college affordability, the resulting plan includes combining Biden's earlier proposal to double the Pell Grant and Sanders's 2017 College for All plan.

This policy is extremely generous to lower-income students. A student at the 10th percentile of income and assets would receive $11,000 from eliminating tuition and a Pell Grant that is double in value, paying an additional $6,345 beyond the current benefit. A student at the 25th percentile would do almost as well. These students were paying an average net price of $12,000 to $14,000 beforehand, including loans and student employment. Under the proposed system, students at the 10th and 25th percentiles would face a negative net price. They would not be required to work or take out loans with an additional \$2,000 to \$5,000 to spare after paying all their college costs, including living expenses.

This proposal also provides the \$11,000 tuition reduction to middle- and upper-middle-class students. They would not be eligible for a Pell Grant even after it doubled in value. Only students at the 90th percentile of the income distribution would not benefit from this policy because of the \$125,000 cap on eligibility for free tuition. Sanders's 2019 plan is the only one that does not include this cap.

One clear benefit that these free college proposals provide is communication. Relative to the continued dilemma of easily communicating pricing under the current financial aid system augmented with a doubled value of the Pell Grant, free college is a much easier "sell." The marketing advantage of this approach, though, comes at the expense of what is a poorly targeted system that provides excessive benefits to students from higher-income families.

Impact on Private Institutions

Aside from these issues of pricing among public universities, the implications of free college for many private universities would be devastating. Reducing the net price of public institutions by \$11,000 for large segments of the college-going student population would put the private institutions at a significant competitive disadvantage. Elite private institutions with large endowments would likely be able to weather the storm. Many of them already have meet-full-need financial aid policies. They may have the market power to maintain their current system of pricing. Relatively few institutions, though, fit into that category.

The rest would need to compete for students by lowering their prices substantially. An important premise of this book is that those institutions are already unable to provide sufficient financial aid to lower-income students because they do not have the market power to charge higher levels of tuition to higher-income students. Their high sticker prices are offset by extensive merit award offers that substantially reduce the price that those students pay. Competition with public institutions drives those pricing policies. If free college lowered the price of public institutions further, private institutions would need to do so as well. The loss of revenue at public institutions would be filled in with funding from taxpayers, but the private institutions have no revenue source to replace those lost funds.

To the extent that public policy has an interest in maintaining the survival of these private institutions, policies like doubling the value of the Pell Grant have an important advantage. Pell Grants provide funding to students regardless of the institution they attend, public or private. The universal nature of these awards does not penalize any category of institution. These private institutions already have a bigger problem with affordability for lower-income students, as documented in chapter 5. Providing them with additional resources to reduce their costs would enable them to do so in a financially sustainable way. Their existence supports a higher-education system that provides students with a greater variety of educational opportunities, enabling them to choose the option that best suits their needs.

Free Community College

Although the focus of this book has been the market for four-year, residential colleges and universities, it is worthwhile to briefly evaluate proposals to make community college tuition free. President Biden advocated for such a policy during the 2020 presidential campaign in his "Plan for Education beyond High School." In this sector of the market, the difference between a free community college policy and doubling the Pell Grant is not that large.

My calculations using IPEDS data (see chapter 1) indicate that the 2018–19 median annual COA (including books, transportation, and other expenses) community colleges charged for state residents living with their family was $9,700; 55 percent of their students currently receive a Pell Grant. Even more students would become eligible for Pell Grants if their value were doubled. At a maximum value of $12,690, those grants would cover a large or complete share of the cost for many of them.

Free college would lead to a similar outcome. If community college tuition, which averaged $4,200 in 2018–19 (again, see chapter 1), was eliminated, even the current level of the Pell Grant would cover the remaining $5,500 COA for eligible students. Free community college would provide additional benefits to community college students who are not eligible for Pell Grants, but a much smaller share of higher-income students. The poor targeting of a broader free college program is less severe here.

One important concern, though, is the extent to which students' enrollment patterns are influenced by the price differential created between community colleges and four-year colleges if only the former is tuition free. Much like research found regarding the Massachusetts Adams Scholarship (Cohodes and Goodman, 2014), students may respond to the policy by enrolling in community colleges instead of four-year colleges (Avery et al., 2019). Community colleges are an appropriate educational outcome for some students, but those who are a better fit for four-year institutions would be better off attending one of them. Free community college may distort those decisions. Doubling the Pell Grant would avoid that issue because it would be available regardless of the level of institution students attend.

Discussion

I began this chapter with the premise that any reasonable policy that would make college more affordable for lower-income students would require charging higher-income individuals more to provide the funding to charge lower-income individuals less. Increasing sticker prices at public institutions that only higher-income students pay would generate necessary funds to provide greater financial aid to lower-income students. It is unlikely, though, that such an approach is politically feasible. In terms of public policy, this requires using a progressive tax system to raise funds to pay for subsidies that lower the cost of college. I focused much of this discussion on two alternative strategies for doing so, doubling the size of the Pell Grant and proposals to make college "free."

Doubling the Pell Grant does a much better job of targeting those students who need the assistance the most. According to my calculations, it is mainly students at the 10th and 25th percentiles of the income/asset distributions who face college costs that are unaffordable. Doubling the Pell Grant solves that problem for these students. Implementing this approach, though, also requires simplifying the system of awarding financial aid to make college pricing more transparent. Creating a pricing system that is affordable for all regardless of income is of no value if nobody understands it.

Free college gets the messaging right, but in my view the pricing system itself leaves something to be desired. My assessment of these plans is that they are overly generous to those higher up the income distribution, for whom college affordability is less of an issue at public institutions. Depending on how it is implemented, it may be extremely generous to lower-income families or it could ignore their issues completely. Joe Biden's 2020 general election plan to combine free college with a doubling of the Pell Grant fits into the first category—it is actually overly generous to lower-income families. The Excelsior Scholarship in New York State fits into the second—it only provides benefits to middle- and upper-middle-income students. Neither seems appropriate. Broader free college proposals also would threaten the existence of many private institutions that do not have large endowments. Overall, free college is an inferior pricing policy relative to doubling the Pell Grant.

CHAPTER SEVEN

Other Barriers to College Access

The focus of this book up to this point has been the system of pricing in higher education and the problems it creates in limiting college access. Other aspects of higher education, though, beyond those directly related to pricing, also impose barriers (Holzer and Baum, 2017). The purpose of this chapter is to provide a brief overview of some of those additional issues. I focus on (a) the excessive levels of student loans and the possibility of defaulting on them, (b) the complexity of the college application process itself and the obstacles students face in navigating it, and (c) the complicated financial aid award letters students receive when accepted at an institution and the difficulties they face in understanding them. Each of these issues complicate students' ability to make wise higher-education decisions.

We can overcome these problems. In fact, some aspects of the student loan problem are based on imperfect information and may not be as serious as some believe, at least for the nonprofit, four-year residential colleges and universities on which I focus in this analysis. This is not to say that there are no problems with the student loan system, but providing better information to clarify the matter for prospective students and policy makers would be helpful in identifying its core. The substantive issues require active intervention to fix them.

The discussion of these topics in this chapter is not intended to be a comprehensive analysis—student loans, for instance, could require a book-length treatment on their own. Yet they are connected to pricing and the financial aid system; briefly addressing them complements the contents of the rest of this book.

Student Loans

It is just as easy to find press reports about the student debt crisis as it is to find reports about the high cost of college (see, for example, Hess, 2020). The main piece of evidence typically cited is the total level of outstanding student loan debt. As of the second quarter of 2020, it stood at $1.54 trillion, higher than any form of debt other than home mortgages (Federal Reserve Bank of New York, 2020). That amount stood at $240 billion in the first quarter of 2003. The rate at which students began repaying their loans within five years of taking them out also fell from 60 percent to 51 percent for those starting college in 2006–7 to 2011–12 (Baum et al., 2019). Stories of students with crippling loan burdens of $100,000 or more are easy to find (see, for instance, Kirst, 2019). These are all staggering numbers and deserving of our attention.

Just as it is possible that concerns about high costs lead to poor decision making among potential college-going students, concerns about high student debt may similarly influence student behavior. Both can limit access if lower-income students withdraw from the college-going process or attend less selective institutions because they are afraid of the cost or the potential loan burden.

Loans at Four-Year Residential Nonprofit Institutions

Much of this book has been devoted to examining the college pricing system and distinguishing where college affordability really is a problem from where misinformation exists. I focused specifically on the market for four-year residential nonprofit colleges in that analysis. The discussion here provides a brief analysis of student loans in the same market. There are clear weaknesses in the system, but the evidence also suggests that some of the concern is misguided, particularly with regard to this segment of the higher-education market.

To assess trends in student loan use, I use data from the Institute for College Access and Success (TICAS, available at https://www.collegein sight.org), which includes institution-level data over time on the average debt held by students when they leave college and the percentage of students who had outstanding debt at that time. Initially, I aggregated institutions into the four categories used throughout the book, weighting averages by enrollment to provide statistics that are representative of

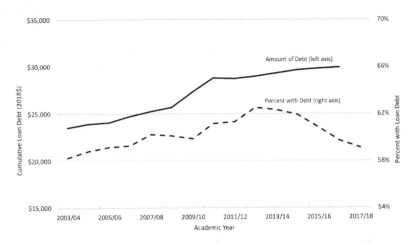

FIGURE 7.1. Percent of students with debt at graduation and average amount of debt at four-year, nonprofit residential colleges (public and private)

Source: Author's calculations based on data available from the Institute for College Access and Success, College Insight, http://college-insight.org. Student debt and undergraduate financial aid data are licensed from Peterson's Undergraduate Financial Aid and Undergraduate Databases, © 2019 Peterson's LLC, all rights reserved. All data may be reproduced, with attribution, subject to restrictions under this Creative Commons license: https://creativecommons .org/licenses/by-nc-nd/3.0/.

students, not institutions. It turns out that the patterns over time in the data across the four institutional categories are similar, so I combine all of them for presentation purposes.

The results of this analysis are displayed in figure 7.1. The dotted line in the figure shows the percentage of students who borrowed while in school. It increased considerably between 2009–10 and 2012–13, which is well timed to the economic damage inflicted on families by the Great Recession. Afterward, borrowing rates fell back to their earlier level as the economy improved. Although not shown here, the likelihood of borrowing at public flagship/R1 institutions and heavily endowed private colleges and universities is lower than it is at the other types of institutions (consistent with the higher income of their students), but the time pattern follows the same path as shown in figure 7.1.

The solid line in the figure displays average debt burden per student. It shows that students borrow more over time, but the increase is slow throughout most of the period other than a steeper ascent between 2008–9 and 2010–11. That period coincides with an increase in student loan borrowing limits in the Federal Direct Student Loan program. That increase took place in 2007–8 for freshman and sophomores and then again in 2008–9 for all students (Black et al., 2020). Students could borrow $17,125 over four years prior to the change and $25,000 afterward. It took a few years for students to take advantage of the full increase in borrowing capacity as they aged through college, and the extended borrowing capacity over this period appears in the data. Otherwise, average debt burdens increased slowly.

Black et al. (2020) find that the greater debt associated with these increased borrowing limits was actually beneficial to students. These authors examine the impact of this policy change on economic outcomes for students who took advantage of the greater availability of federal loan funding (although not specifically focused on the institutions I consider). They also find that student debt rose as loan limits increased. They go on to show that those loans were used to improve students' educational outcomes, resulting in a greater likelihood of completing a degree, higher subsequent earnings, and a greater likelihood of repaying those loans. Overall, the data presented in figure 7.1 and this additional evidence suggest that student debt is not a growing problem in the market for four-year residential nonprofit colleges.

Problems with Loans in the Broader College Market

Problems with student loans, though, do exist; they are just more relevant for a different slice of the higher-education market. Looney and Yannelis (2015) point to the for-profit and community college sectors that have contributed to a dour student loan landscape. Much of the growth in loans has occurred in these institutions, and default rates are high among students who attend them. The problem at these institutions is that students borrow to enroll, but the returns are lower there. At community colleges, the problem is the low graduation rates. Baum et al. (2019) show that repayment rates for those who borrow to attend community college are relatively high if they complete their degree but low otherwise. At for-profit institutions, even those who complete the program often struggle in the labor market, leading to low repayment rates.

Certainly, some students borrow large amounts of money to fund an education that is not "worth it," and these stories receive considerable attention. But the data show that those who borrow the most are also the ones most likely to pay back their debts (Brown et al., 2015; Looney, 2020). The trouble spot in the student loan market appears to be the smaller loans made to students who attend community colleges who do not graduate, or loans made to students to attend for-profit institutions.

The Bigger Picture on Student Loans

Taking a step back from the data, it is useful to keep in mind the ways in which loans can fit into a sensible financial plan for students. I have discussed the role of higher education in developing human capital in the same way that firms acquire physical capital as an approach to improve their productivity. It is usually the case when a firm chooses to do so, it borrows money to smooth the flow of financing for, say, a machine that will provide benefits for many years.

Likewise, a college education increases productivity and earnings for potentially the rest of a student's work life. Conceptually, there is nothing wrong with the notion of borrowing to finance that investment. I provided evidence in chapter 3 about the high return to a college education, well beyond its cost, on average, and plausibly worthy of borrowing to finance it.

Problems with loans arise when institutions promote degree programs with lower payoffs. This is an example where government regulation could help students, particularly in the context of for-profit institutions (Cellini, 2020). Community colleges provide valuable returns for those who graduate (Marcotte, 2019), but public policy should address ways to increase completion (Dawson, Kearney, and Sullivan, 2020). Greater reliance on income-based repayment programs also could help (Dynarski, 2016). Fixing the problems associated with college pricing would also be beneficial. If we were able to make college more affordable for lower-income students as I have proposed in this book, they would not need to borrow as much. Overall, though, if borrowing supports smart educational investments, it should not be discouraged.

Navigating the Application Process

Obstacles in the College Application Process

Applying to college is no simple task. The focus of this book has been the problems that the pricing system introduces into the process, but it is obvious that it is not the only sticking point. The first difficulty is doing well in school, an issue that is beyond the scope of this book. But students that are on the college track still have a long road ahead of them. Aside from evaluating costs, they need to consider what they want to study, what types of schools would be a good fit for them, what tests they need to take (AP/SAT/ACT), how to prepare for those tests, how to apply, how to evaluate their options if and when they are accepted, how to prepare to begin college, and other steps I almost certainly left out here. The college-going process is more like competing in the fifteen hundred meters and the high hurdles combined—it requires endurance and the ability to overcome substantial obstacles along the way.

This process is hard enough for students with resources, which could come in the form of higher family income or parents, friends, or relatives who have gone through it themselves—the two often go together. Without those resources, it is a daunting challenge. Even if we could convince these students that college is affordable, that may not be enough to get them through the process and make good college decisions.

In theory, students all have their high school counselors to help. But school counselors are burdened with heavy caseloads, averaging 430 students per counselor nationwide. Caseloads in Arizona (905), California (612), Illinois (626), Michigan (691), and Minnesota (654) are well beyond that according to the American School Counselor Association (2020). Expecting school counselors to provide those services is unrealistic.

This problem is also clear based on the number of other providers of comprehensive application assistance. High-income families often hire advisers. Some students from lower-income families and those who are the first in their families to attend college (first generation) are fortunate to receive these services from nonprofit organizations. These include groups like College Advising Corps, College Possible, UAspire, and others. These organizations are designed to help students overcome all the hurdles described previously by assigning students to individual advisers.

The Effectiveness of Application Support Services

The educational impact of nonprofit programs like these is reviewed in Page and Scott-Clayton (2016). These authors focus on evidence that relies on randomized controlled trials (RCTs) and other interventions that approximate the idea of a controlled experiment, so-called quasi experiments like those described earlier in this book. Carrell and Sacerdote (2017) represents an example of such an RCT. They find that students randomly assigned to a treatment group receiving coaching/mentoring services focusing on the college application process were more likely to attend college and persist while there. Taken as a whole, this body of research shows that such programs can increase college enrollment overall, particularly enrollment at four-year colleges and universities, and institutions that better match a student's academic ability.

One weakness I have noted firsthand in the college-advising process is the limited information on financial aid available to these students. The advisers themselves face the same difficulty as others in communicating college affordability. They have the advantage of telling students that college will be more affordable than they think, and the students believe them because they have formed a relationship. Advisers would still benefit if they could provide accurate and more detailed pricing information that could help break down that barrier. The pricing changes I propose in this book are completely complementary with these types of interventions.

Page and Scott-Clayton (2016) similarly review the evidence of other forms of lower-intensity interventions designed to help students navigate a part of the college application process. In chapter 4, I reviewed an example of this research (Bettinger et al., 2012), describing the results from the H&R Block FAFSA experiment. In that intervention, participants were randomly assigned to a control group, one treatment group that was given information about their eligibility for federal financial aid, or a second treatment group that also received assistance applying for that aid. No other services were provided. Again, it was the cost information combined with assistance that made the difference.

Several other less-intensive interventions have been tested that are designed to facilitate the application process for lower-income and first-generation students that also have an impact on college-going decisions. These include "nudges" designed to remind students to meet certain deadlines (Castleman and Page, 2015; Avery et al., 2020) and programs enabling lower-income students to send test scores to schools for free (Pallais, 2015). These interventions have been found to be successful in many instances at encouraging college enrollment.

The existence of these different types of programs highlights the broader set of constraints beyond price that students face in the college-going process. It is likely that improving access to college to the broadest possible population will require a comprehensive approach that includes many of these types of interventions. My focus on pricing is just one component. I believe it is a critical part, though, because of the extent to which it interacts with these other approaches.

The Role of Award Letters

You have completed 1,480 of the 1,500 meters of the race and you are approaching the finish line. Suddenly, an unexpected hurdle pops up that you need to overcome to complete it. It is the financial aid award letter that you receive from each college to which you have been accepted. It is called a financial aid award letter because, in theory, it tells students exactly how much financial aid they have been "awarded" and how much they will have to pay themselves. Students need this information to determine exactly how much they will pay for their education and to compare final pricing across institutions. Can they afford to attend? Is another suitable institution a more cost-effective option?

The problem is that the information in this letter is also difficult to understand. For months or perhaps years of confusion regarding what college is really going to cost, students finally arrive at the moment when the mystery should be solved. All the facts should be on the table at this point, and students can use the exact, actual cost to inform their final decision. Then they open the award letter, and a resolution eludes them. It does not provide the information they need, and each school's letter is formatted in its own way with somewhat different information presented. The confusion continues.

A Sample Award Letter

To illustrate the problem, table 7.1 provides an example of a financial aid award letter that I found online (modified slightly, changing labels to avoid identifying the institution). First, what are all these items listed under "Your Financial Aid Award" and why do I need to "accept" them? The scholarships are listed for two reasons. First, they are relevant to the institution in terms of budgeting—that is where the money will come from that is covering the cost. That is not relevant to the student. If those scholarships are merit awards, though, they also satisfy the marketing goals of providing these awards. I have addressed the downsides of these awards in the higher-education market in the context of a prisoners' dilemma in chapter 2. Students are then asked to indicate their loan amount when an amount is listed. They are told they can borrow a different amount, but how should they determine that?

In the bottom portion of the letter, students are told their estimated cost of attendance (COA), broken down by type of expense. Reporting

TABLE 7.1. Sample financial aid award letter

Your Financial Aid Award	Amount	Accept (Y/N)	Loan Amount*
Douglas L. Powell Scholarship	$14,000	_____	
Janet T. Yellen Scholarship	$14,926	_____	
Benjamin G. Bernanke Scholarship	$11,904	_____	
Federal Pell Grant	$4,770	_____	
Direct Subsidized Loan	$3,500	_____	_____
Direct Unsubsidized Loan	$2,000	_____	_____
Federal Work-Study	$2,500	_____	
Award Total	**$53,600**		

*You may request a different loan amount, but please pay attention to the annual loan limits based on your class level. (Refer to the general information sheet.) Subsidized loan and work-study eligibility are based on estimates and may change once your FAFSA results have been reviewed. Work-study should not be used in calculating your payment. Work-study wages are paid directly to the student.

Estimated Cost of Attendance (COA)		**Expected Family Contribution (EFC)**	
Tuition and Fees	$49,780	Parent Contribution	$5,205
Room and Board	$12,524	Student Contribution	$2,144
Books and Incidentals	$1,400		
Travel	$250		
Total COA	**$63,954**	**Total EFC**	**$7,349**
		Financial Need (COA – EFC)	**$56,605**

the full COA (sticker price) is perhaps of little value, since that is not what the student will pay, but it is useful for students to see an estimated budget for the things they will need to spend their money on, like books.

The real difficulty in this award is the part that matters the most: What does the student actually have to pay? It turns out that this piece of information is not included in the award letter, despite the fact that it probably is the number that students and their families want to see the most. One might think that the amount the family has to pay is the expected family contribution (EFC). That amount is listed as $7,349. It is broken down into a student and parent contribution, but it is not clear why the family cares about that.

Regardless, that is not what the student/family has to pay. The COA is listed as $63,954, and the financial aid award is listed as $53,600 (including loans and work-study). I would interpret the information in this award as indicating that the student/family owe $10,354 out of pocket (COA less financial aid, which includes grant aid, loans, and work-study). That number does not appear anywhere on this form. Since that payment is greater than the student's EFC of $7,349, that would indicate that this institution does not meet full need.

It is troubling that I am seven chapters into a book describing the details of the financial aid process, and I am not positive that this is how much this student will have to pay to attend this college. The family cannot find this information straightforward. I think the college is asking this student to pay

$10,354   out-of-pocket cost

$5,500   student loans (including both subsidized and unsubsidized federal
            loans)

$2,500   student employment (work-study)

$18,354   net price.

That is what the family needs to know. It is far from clear in this letter. My assessment is that the family who received it would have no idea how much they are going to have to pay to attend this school.

What an Award Letter Should Include

Ignoring the specifics of this sample award letter, it would be useful to step back and think about what information such a letter really needs to convey. The college has a sticker price. The student will not pay that amount but something less than that. How much will the family pay? These payments will include cash, loans, and student earnings (work-study). These forms of payment are not identical. What students need to know is how much they are expected to borrow, how much they are expected to pay based on employment, and how large a check will they and/or their parents need to write? If the award letter does not easily answer those three fundamental questions of the student in an understandable way, it has failed.

The Institute for College Access and Success (2017) has operationalized these issues in a more formal approach. They argue that these letters need to (1) provide the full COA, (2) separate aid that needs to be earned or repaid from aid that does not, and (3) calculate the net price.

These goals are sensible. Indicating the full COA is less useful itself as much as it is for the subcategories of expenses it includes, like room and board, books, and transportation expenses. It can help students evaluate prospective budgets for living while in college. Separating forms of aid is obvious based on my simpler expression of goals. Personally, I prefer reporting loans, work-study, and cash payments separately. They can be combined into a single net price value to facilitate comparisons across institutions, but the individual elements are the concepts families are more likely to understand.

TICAS examined award letters from almost two hundred public and private nonprofit institutions. They report that only 7 percent contained all three elements.

Alternative Models

The problem associated with complicated award letters is becoming better understood, and steps have been made to improve them. TICAS recommends that all institutions use the format of the US Department of Education's College Financing Plan Template, available online at https://www2.ed.gov/policy/highered/guid/aid-offer/collfinplantemplate.pdf.

Personally, I prefer the template prepared by the American Talent Initiative, displayed in figure 7.2. It highlights right across the top the important math that COA less grants equals net price. It breaks up that net price into the amount that the student needs to pay to the college or university compared to separate expenses like books and transportation. It indicates the parts of those expenses that can be paid by loans or student employment, such as a work-study job. It even indicates how much the check to the college or university would need to be (although that information could be presented more clearly in my view). One could quibble about the exact format of this award letter template, but the idea and execution is far ahead of typical letters currently used. Introducing a uniform format would also be beneficial to help students compare prices across institutions and for counselors and advisers to easily interpret the results. It would be a step forward.

Discussion

We have a long way to go to make the college-going process efficient. Most of this book has focused narrowly on pricing, and that is certainly a critical component of the process. Students need to better understand

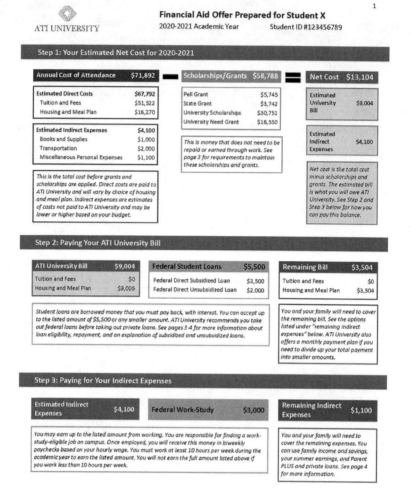

FIGURE 7.2. American Talent Initiative proposed award letter template

pricing, we need to make it easier for them to do so, and for lower-income students we need to find ways to lower the cost.

But we also need to do more. We need to convey that a modest amount of borrowing is a reasonable component of a system that provides affordable educational opportunities. Although some students are borrowing too much, most students attending four-year residential nonprofit institutions are not. We need to be careful in distinguishing where the problem in the loan market really lies.

The rest of the college application process is sufficiently daunting that it opens the door for service providers to help manage the process for lower-income students. Those providers have proven to be effective, but helping them navigate the pricing system with their students would be beneficial.

And award letters need to do a better job of communicating the actual financial aid award so that students understand what they will actually have to pay once they get accepted at an institution. Pricing information needs to be accessible all the way through the process if we are to support access among lower-income students. At each stage better pricing information would be helpful.

Conclusion

What College Access Means to Families

As I explained in the introduction, my personal experiences—and difficulties—navigating the college pricing system led me to dive into the world of financial aid. As a professional economist, my initial instinct was to collect data and crunch numbers, which I did. The first "deliverable" from my efforts was a working prototype of a simplified financial aid estimator for Wellesley College, which existed at that time in the form of an Excel spreadsheet.

What really solidified my understanding of the problems in the financial aid system, though, came after that. The admissions and financial aid staff at Wellesley College, who were incredibly supportive partners throughout the process, set up focus groups to test the prototype. Prospective students and their parents who came to campus for a tour and information session were asked to stay afterward to discuss financial aid if they were interested. We would then hand them an iPad with the spreadsheet on it and ask them if they would like to get an estimate of what they might expect to pay to attend Wellesley based on the parents' basic income and assets.

That experience drove home for me what this was all about. It was difficult to tell by looking at them the financial status of those in the room, but what was clear to me was the anxiety they all felt about the cost. All parents want the best for their children. They want to be able to give them the best educational experience possible, if only they can afford it. All the prospective students looked at their parents almost begging for the answer to be yes (presumably if they stayed for this additional session, they were still interested in attending Wellesley).

Wellesley College happens to fall into the category of highly endowed private colleges that now charges a sticker price around $75,000 but also meets students' full financial need. Parents were petrified. The ones who stayed knew they could not afford the sticker price. I would watch a parent type in their finances and watch Excel do its instantaneous magic in calculating the results. Then came the response—typically words were not spoken but the immediate tension release was palpable. The weight of the world appeared to lift off their shoulders. They could do for their children what they wanted. It might not be easy. It would still be a struggle, but it was possible. Regardless of the type of institution, every child and every parent deserve that experience.

College pricing is not the only factor that restricts access for lower-income families, but it is certainly an important one. It is a lost opportunity if students do not attend because they think they cannot afford it. There are plenty of obstacles in the United States that interfere with a student getting to the point of being college ready. But those who are should be given that chance to attend college and one that is the right fit for them. It may be the linchpin that elevates their economic standing for the rest of their lives and perhaps the lives of their children after that. This is a problem that we must solve.

Review of the Book

This book has focused on the pricing system in American higher education and identified three main problems: (1) attending college costs less than people think; (2) colleges do a poor job of communicating those costs, leading to the confusion; and (3) the actual price is still too high for lower-income families at most institutions.

I have also explored the market factors that contribute to the problems in the current pricing system, focusing on competition between institutions and the existence of public and private systems. Seeking to maintain affordability, public institutions set a low sticker price even though that amount is paid only by higher-income families. This restricts revenue that can be used to reduce the price to an affordable level for lower-income students. Greater state funding often leads to lower sticker prices, not more financial aid. Private colleges other than the few highly selective institutions with very large endowments find themselves at a competitive disadvantage. Despite their high sticker prices, these institutions offer significant discounts for students from higher-income families in the form of merit awards to compete with public institutions. This restricts their revenue. Without other sources of funding available, they do not have the ability to charge lower-income students an affordable price.

I have also argued in this book that the solution to these problems requires dedicating more resources to reduce the price for lower-income students. The two main viable policy options today are doubling the size of the Pell Grant or introducing a free college policy. I reviewed those alternatives in detail in chapter 6, concluding that doubling the Pell Grant is a more targeted approach that closes the affordability gap in college costs faced by students from lower-income families. Pursuing this path, though, requires a system that does a far better job of communicating pricing. An appropriately configured free college program could also close that gap at public institutions, but it unnecessarily benefits those further up the income distribution and places the finances of private higher-education institutions without large endowments at serious risk.

Introducing the Affordable College Act (ACA2)

In the introduction, I drew parallels between problems in the health care market and the higher-education market related to access and pricing. I revisit that comparison now to consider policy responses and offer additional insights in the market for higher education.

Individuals receive health care services from insurance providers from both the public and private sectors in the United States. Traditionally, many individuals received health insurance through Medicare (generally those over age 65) or Medicaid (mainly lower-income families), which are provided by the government. Others received private insurance, received mainly through their jobs.

The purpose of the Affordable Care Act (ACA), enacted in 2010, is to increase the health insurance coverage of individuals who would previously be uninsured. Most employers now are mandated to provide coverage. The Medicaid system was expanded to cover those with incomes up to 133 percent of the poverty level; previously the limit was much lower than that (differing by state). Others who do not fit in these categories, like self-employed individuals, are offered insurance through government-run insurance exchanges that provide insurance plans with premiums tied to the individual's income. Twenty million individuals who would have been uninsured otherwise are now covered by health insurance because of the ACA (Gruber and Sommers, 2019).

The current policy debate in the Democratic Party is about whether moving toward universal health care requires tweaks to the ACA (like the "public option") or a complete overhaul of the system. Proposals to provide Medicare for All typically include provisions to eliminate private insurance and cover all Americans under a single government-run plan.

In terms of higher education, the two proposals I focus on to make college more affordable are analogous to the ACA/Medicare for All debate. Free college is the conceptual equivalent of Medicare for All. It represents an extensive overhaul in terms of the way in which students finance their college education similar to how Medicare for All would overhaul the health care financing system. Those who have less access to the system would now get it for free. Those who already have access to the system would now get it in a different way, with perhaps additional subsidies. There is a trade-off between a universal system and one that provides benefits to those who already receive those services.

Making college cheaper for students from lower-income families by doubling the value of the Pell Grant is the conceptual equivalent of the ACA. It largely works within the existing structure of the system, making it easier for those who currently have trouble accessing the system to receive those services. I think of the proposal to double the maximum value of the Pell Grant as ACA2, the Affordable College Act. The centerpiece of the ACA2 would be the Pell Grant increase, but that would need to be implemented with a better approach at communicating college costs (if a tree falls in the forest . . .). As I argued earlier, I support this ACA2.

Final Thoughts

In the end, what we are looking for is a way to ease the anxiety and lift the weight off the shoulders of students and their parents, as I observed in my focus groups. A college education is an investment that generates substantial returns. It does not need to be free. It just needs to be affordable, not just for the rich but for everyone. When we can introduce a system where that is true and where everyone knows what to expect, we will have accomplished the goal of making college accessible. Regardless of resources, every student can attend the institution that is the right fit. If we can do that, the system will be just.

Acknowledgments

It is customary in a book project like this to express gratitude to all the individuals who helped bring the book to fruition. Colleagues whose discussions and comments on drafts helped shape the content, research assistants who did a lot of the truly difficult but often less exciting work, friends and family who provided the personal support necessary to enable the author to engage in the process, the editor who guided the author through it, and others. It goes without saying that no book can be completed without this form of support, and all those who provide it deserve much more than a line in an acknowledgments section. I will also follow this custom below.

But writing this book was a bit different for me. Not only did I require assistance from others in its production, but I benefited tremendously from dozens of individuals who first brought me to the place where I could even imagine thinking about writing a book like this. As I indicate elsewhere, fifteen years ago I knew very little about financial aid. My interest piqued when my children were approaching college age and I realized how complicated the system was (and is). It has been quite a journey getting from that place to where I am today. Much of it involved my experiences developing MyinTuition; those involved in that process will be featured prominently in this discussion. I would be remiss not to acknowledge their contributions in teaching me what I now know about financial aid, which helped me reach the point where I could write this book. I will express my gratitude to them based on the chronology of their inputs rather than their importance, since everyone in this discussion was incredibly influential to me. All individuals are or were affiliated with Wellesley College except as noted.

I first met Kim Bottomly in a "get to know you" meeting after she had been appointed president of Wellesley College in 2007 (she stepped down from that position in 2016). When I happened to mention the problems I experienced navigating the financial aid system with my children, she suggested I consider doing something about it. She volunteered college data, resources, and funding to promote my efforts. Without that push, nothing that followed could have happened. We launched MyinTuition at Wellesley College because of those efforts. When other institutions expressed interest in adopting it, Kim was clear that any other school could do so without having to worry about paying royalties. The goal of providing transparency in pricing and increasing access to college was important enough that MyinTuition needed to be as widely available as possible. It exemplified the college's motto: "Non Ministrari sed Ministrare" (Not to be ministered unto, but to minister).

Kim started the ball rolling, but then the education process began. Kathy Osmond was the financial aid director at that time. I recall meeting with her in front of her computer screen as she described the components of a financial aid record and how all the data gathered gets used to determine a financial aid award. It was an eye-opening (and a bit scarring!) experience. Learning how to simplify the process required understanding what was under the hood in the first place, and Kathy provided me with that background.

The next step was data acquisition. How do I access the extensive financial detail in the database and figure out how to boil it down to more manageable components? Mary Roberts was the individual in the financial aid office at that time responsible for data management. Mary and I worked closely together to try and figure out what data were available and what data I would want and need. Anyone who has seen the pages of field names (in Banner) that begin with RCRAPP, RORSTAT, and others will know how difficult this exercise was and can appreciate the value of Mary's contributions as she guided me through it brilliantly. Ron LeShane eventually took over these tasks from Mary, and his assistance has also been incredibly helpful.

Eventually it became time to move out from the backroom and start thinking about a public-facing product. What do prospective students and their parents care about? What do they know and understand? What will be most meaningful for them? This is when it became time to engage with the admissions and financial aid professionals who deal with these issues on a daily basis.

I cannot say enough about the value of the contributions made in this process by Jenn Desjarlais (vice president for admissions and financial aid at that time), Joy St. John (director of admissions at that time and now vice president for admissions and financial aid), and Scott Wallace-Juedes (director of financial aid at that time and now director of undergraduate financial aid at Yale University). We spent hours (weeks! months!) together talking about these issues (including a lengthy discussion about the difference between the words "cost" and "price," which I will never forget!). We developed the language used in MyinTuition to be as accessible as possible to students and families without violating essential financial aid principles. We tested prototypes to gauge student response. We gave talks to professional audiences about MyinTuition and its potential role in improving pricing transparency and college access. I learned a tremendous amount about the financial aid world from this group (we sometimes referred to ourselves as the "Dream Team"). Not only were my interactions with them incredibly valuable professionally, but they were also very enjoyable at a personal level. I miss regularly working with them.

By this point in the development of MyinTuition, significant staff resources were devoted to launching the tool and making it successful. Ravi Ravishanker, the chief technology officer, wrote the code himself to make it run on the college's website. Much of the public affairs staff were involved in launching and promoting it. Elizabeth Gildersleeve (chief communications officer at that time) oversaw the effort along with Sofiya Cabalquinto (senior director of communications at that time). Colette Porter (director of campaign communications at that time) and Julie Turner (assistant director of marketing communications) led much of the marketing activities. Jane Kyricos (from admissions, now retired) chipped in to the marketing effort. Soe Lin Post (director of design) contributed both the MyinTuition graphic and even deserves credit for coming up with the name! Cameran Mason (chief development officer) was also a big supporter. Beyond the incredible productivity that this team provided, I am also grateful to all of them for the friendships that evolved over the course of this work.

By 2017, MyinTuition left the Wellesley College environment and formed its own nonprofit organization. I hired Dan Richards to serve as my chief technology officer. Dan is my right-hand man. Nothing happens in my work without his input. I know a lot about numbers and, by now, a lot about the way the financial aid system works, but how that knowledge translates into a tool that hundreds of thousands of students use per year at dozens of colleges and universities only happens because Dan knows how to do that. He leads our team that includes programmers and a website designer (Danica Cheslofska, who does a great job!). Without him,

I could not have continued down this path, and I am grateful for that. Along with Corinna Graham, our social media adviser, we have an outstanding team that works together effectively in support of a mission that we all believe in. Andy Evans and Carol Herman add even greater support in the form of their service on our board of directors (along with Dan Richards and Kristin Butcher), and I am extremely grateful for their thoughtful input.

The advantage of working with dozens of colleges and universities with MyinTuition is that I have access to the admissions and financial aid directors and staff at all of them. Discussing with them what my tool offers, what they want it to offer, and why their institutional environment may be a bit different than others has been an incredible education into the broader world of financial aid. These schools include highly selective and heavily endowed private institutions, tuition-dependent private institutions, and public institutions. The issues these different types of institutions face are not the same, as one might expect. Working with each of them has provided me with insights that would be difficult to garner without this insider's perspective.

Many of the individuals at these institutions have made contributions that deserve acknowledgment. John Gudvangen, associate vice chancellor for financial aid at the University of Denver, for instance, has provided invaluable insights that go beyond just the issues he faces at his institution. He has served as a useful sounding board for ideas I have had about the system, and I have learned a lot from him. Individuals at early adopters of MyinTuition were also influential. To name a few of them (hoping not to offend the many others who certainly were incredibly helpful as well!), this group includes: Gail Holt (Amherst), Mike Bartini (Bowdoin), Jim Tilton (Brown), Rod Oto (Carleton), Jill Pierce (Colby), Gina Soliz (Colgate), Kim Downs (Middlebury), Anne Walker (Rice), Stephanie DuPaul (Richmond), Audrey Smith (Smith), Carly Eichhorst (St. Olaf), Scott Miller (UVA), Bob Coughlin (Wesleyan), Paul Boyer (Williams), and Jeremiah Quinlan (Yale). At more recent adopters, Kathy Lynch (UMass Boston) and Kevin Lamb (Centre) have been very helpful. Again, this list is too short, but all the administrators in admissions and financial aid at all the institutions I work with at MyinTuition have provided me with valuable contributions to my financial aid education. This book would not have happened without them.

More recently, I have turned my attention toward conducting academic research on the topic of college access and financial aid. Those efforts are captured in this book. I am grateful to Jennifer Ma (College Board) and Lauren Russell (University of Pennsylvania) for collaborating with me on a project focused on directly identifying the existence of sticker shock. As this book is being completed, I am just beginning work on a project with Dubravka Ritter (Federal Reserve Bank of Philadelphia and a former student!) on the role that wealth inequality plays in the financial aid system. I am hopeful that effort results in a better understanding of its potential limitations.

Now I turn to the people who actually helped me specifically with this book! Again, it takes a village to undertake a project of this scope, and several people were incredibly helpful in bringing this book to fruition. The individual who deserves extra special recognition is Emily Cloonan. She is a student who enrolled at Wellesley College in the fall of 2019. She never took one of my classes, but when I advertised for the position of summer research assistant, she applied. I hired her because she worked in the financial aid office that year and had an interest in and familiarity with the issues the book addresses. Of course, the summer of 2020 involved no in-person interactions of any kind because of COVID-19. Emily did all her work for me remotely, and we met over Zoom.

Perhaps it was not the ideal environment to be conducting summer research, but her work effort was incredibly valuable to me. Emily's main task was to obtain the net price calculator estimates used in much of this book. We obtained estimates for two hundred schools and five income/asset categories, so that is one thousand sets of entries into net price calculators. For those of you who know the difficulty of navigating those tools, you will understand the contribution to this project that Emily made! It was demanding work that she undertook, and she did an excellent job. Without Emily, there would be no book! Emily has since transferred to Georgetown, a true loss for Wellesley College.

I also owe an incredible debt of gratitude to those individuals who discussed the content of the book with me and read earlier drafts to help me refine my arguments. Kristin Butcher, Robin McKnight, and Melissa Kearney (all economists, colleagues, and good friends) read and commented on all or most of the first full draft before the book was sent out for external review. After the reviews were received and I incorporated the reviewers' comments, I called on Joy St. John, Paul Boyer (a recently retired financial aid director from Williams College who I worked with at an early stage of MyinTuition), and Samantha Heep (one of my former and very smart economics students at Wellesley who also happens to write very well). All of them graciously volunteered their time and added additional insights that are incorporated into this final product. The book is much better for their contributions.

I was also fortunate to receive comments from two outstanding reviewers, who are unknown to me. One of them clearly is a scholar who has studied the financial aid system extensively. This individual's detailed insights that both addressed technical points and issues with coverage of material and packaging were invaluable. They may have been the best set of reviewer comments I have ever received. The second review came from a self-identified financial aid director who had retired some years earlier. This reviewer made the astute comment that I should have an active or very recently retired financial aid director read the book to make sure that the finer points of the financial aid system were characterized accurately. That reviewer was completely correct, and that is what brought me to Paul Boyer.

My editor on this book, Chad Zimmerman, did a yeoman's job of navigating the process that brought this book to completion. I have written books before, but infrequently enough that I very much appreciated his helpful guiding hand. He organized the process and let it unfold in a way that was largely seamless to me, which is what I wanted! I just focused on the writing.

And last, but not least, of course, is my family. As I mentioned in the preface, this entire book was written through the COVID-19 work-from-home era. I do not even want to think about how many hours I spent in my office clicking away on the keys of my laptop. My wife, Heidi, also stuck at home through this period, would come in and, after realizing that my head was in a totally different place in those moments, turn around and leave. Now that this book is complete and the pandemic is winding down (or at least seemed to be briefly), my head will likely still be in the clouds some of the time (OK, maybe a lot of time—it is an occupational hazard), but hopefully less of the time! I am looking forward to returning to our regular life together.

My children, Jake and Noah, are now grown and independent (well, largely!). This book could not have been completed during a pandemic otherwise. They are both on a good path for which I am grateful, freeing up reserve space in my brain to focus on writing this book. They also bring us tremendous pride and joy.

References

Adam, Thomas, and A. Burcu Bayram, eds. 2019. *The Economics of Higher Education in the United States*. College Station: Texas A&M University Press.

Akee, Randall. 2019. "Voting and Income." Econofact. https://econofact.org/voting-and-income, accessed 5/21/2020.

American School Counselor Association. 2020. Student-to-School-Counselor Ratio 2018–2019. Alexandria, VA: American School Counselor Association. https://www.schoolcounselor.org/getmedia/c0351f10-45d1-4812-9c88-85b071628bb4/Ratios18-19.pdf, accessed 8/16/2021.

Angrist, Joshua, David Autor, Sally Hudson, and Amanda Pallais. 2014. "Leveling Up: Early Results from a Randomized Evaluation of Postsecondary Aid." National Bureau of Economic Research, NBER Working Paper 20800. Cambridge, MA: National Bureau of Economic Research.

———. 2016. "Evaluating Post-Secondary Aid: Enrollment, Persistence, and Projected Completion Effects." NBER Working Paper 23015. Cambridge, MA: National Bureau of Economic Research.

Angrist, Joshua, David Autor, and Amanda Pallais. 2020. "Marginal Effects of Merit Aid for Low-Income Students." NBER Working Paper 27834. Cambridge, MA: National Bureau of Economic Research.

Archibald, Robert B., and David H. Feldman. 2014. *Why Does College Cost So Much?* New York: Oxford University Press.

———. 2016. *Federal Financial Aid Policy and College Behavior*. Washington, DC: American Council on Education.

Avery, Christopher, Benjamin L. Castleman, Michael Hurwitz, Bridget T. Long, and Lindsay C. Page. 2020. "Digital Messaging to Improve College Enrollment and Success." National Bureau of Economic Research Working Paper 27897.

Avery, Christopher, Jessica Howell, Matea Pender, and Bruce Sacerdote. 2019. "Policies and Payoffs to Addressing America's College Graduation Deficit." *Brookings Papers on Economic Activity*, Fall: 93–149.

Baum, Sandy. 2019. *Rethinking Federal Work-Study: Incremental Reform Is Not Enough*. Washington, DC: Urban Institute.

Baum, Sandy, Jennifer Ma, Matea Pender, and C. J. Libassi. 2019. *Trends in Student Aid 2019*. New York: College Board.

Belley, Philippe, and Lance Lochner. 2007. "The Changing Role of Family Income and Ability in Determining Educational Achievement." *Journal of Human Capital* 1(1): 37–89.

Bennett, William J. 1987. "Our Greedy Colleges." *New York Times*, February 18. https://www.nytimes.com/1987/02/18/opinion/our-greedy-colleges.html, accessed 11/28/2020.

Bettinger, Eric, Oded Gurantz, Laura Kawano, Bruce Sacerdote, and Michael Stevens. 2019. "The Long-Run Impacts of Financial Aid: Evidence from California's Cal Grant." *American Economic Journal: Economic Policy* 11(1): 64–94.

Bettinger, Eric P., Bridget Terry Long, Philip Oreopoulos, and Lisa Sanbonmatsu. 2012. "The Role of Application Assistance and Information in College Decisions: Results from the H&R Block FAFSA Experiment." *Quarterly Journal of Economics* 127(3):1205–42.

Black, Sandra E., Jeffrey T. Denning, and Jesse Rothstein. 2020. "Winners and Losers? The Effect of Gaining and Losing Access to Selective Colleges on Education and Labor Market Outcomes." NBER Working Paper 26821.

Black, Sandra E., Jeffrey T. Denning, Lisa J. Dettling, Sarena Goodman, and Lesley J. Turner. 2020. "Taking It to the Limit: Effects of Increased Student Loan Availability on Attainment, Earnings, and Financial Well-Being." NBER Working Paper 27658.

Bleemer, Zachary. 2020. "Top Percent Policies and the Return to Postsecondary Selectivity." Unpublished manuscript, University of California, Berkeley.

Bleemer, Zachary, and Basit Zafar. 2018. "Intended College Attendance: Evidence from an Experiment on College Returns and Costs." *Journal of Public Economics* 157(1): 184–211.

Blinder, Alan. 1988. *Hard Heads, Soft Hearts: Tough-Minded Economics for a Just Society*. Princeton, NJ: Basic Books.

Boatman, Angela, Brent J. Evans, and Adela Soliz. 2017. "Understanding Loan Aversion in Education: Evidence from High School Seniors, Community College Students, and Adults." *AERA Open* 3(1).

Brown, Meta, Andrew F. Haughwout, Donghoon Lee, Joelle Scally, and Wilbert van der Klaauw. 2015. "Looking at Student Loan Defaults through a Larger Window." New York: Federal Reserve Bank of New York. https://liberty streeteconomics.newyorkfed.org/2015/02/looking_at_student_loan_defaults _through_a_larger_window.html, accessed 8/10/2020.

Card, David. 1999. "The Causal Effect of Education on Earnings." In *Handbook of Labor Economics*, ed. Orley Ashenfelter and David Card, vol. 3, part 1, 1801–63. Amsterdam: Elsevier Science.

Carrell, Scott, and Bruce Sacerdote. 2017. "Why Do College-Going Interventions Work?" *American Economic Journal: Applied Economics* 9(3): 124–51.

Carruthers, Celeste K., William F. Fox, and Christopher Jepsen. 2020. "Promise Kept? Free Community College, Attainment, and Earnings in Tennessee." Unpublished manuscript.

Castleman, Benjamin L., and Bridget Terry Long. 2016. "Looking beyond Enrollment: The Causal Effect of Need-Based Grants on College Access, Persistence, and Graduation." *Journal of Labor Economics* 34(4): 1023–73.

Castleman, Ben, and Lindsay C. Page. 2015. "Summer Nudging: Can Personalized Text Messages and Peer Mentor Outreach Increase College Going among Low-Income High School Graduates?" *Journal of Economic Behavior and Organization* 115: 144–60.

Cellini, Stephani Riegg. 2020. "The Alarming Rise in For-Profit College Enrollment." Washington, DC: Brookings Institution. https://www.brookings.edu/blog/brown-center-chalkboard/2020/11/02/the-alarming-rise-in-for-profit-college-enrollment/, accessed 11/24/2020.

Chakrabarti, Rajashri, Nicole Gorton, and Michael F. Lovenheim. 2020. "State Investment in Higher Education: Effects on Human Capital Formation, Student Debt, and Long-Term Financial Outcomes of Students." National Bureau of Economic Research, NBER Working Paper 27885. Cambridge, MA: National Bureau of Economic Research.

Chetty, Raj, John N. Friedman, Emmanuel Saez, Nicholas Turner, and Danny Yagan. 2020. "Income Segregation and Intergenerational Mobility across Colleges in the United States." *Quarterly Journal of Economics* 135(3): 1567–1633.

Cohodes, Sarah R., and Joshua S. Goodman. 2014. "Merit Aid, College Quality, and College Completion: Massachusetts' Adams Scholarship as an In-Kind Subsidy." *American Economic Journal: Applied Economics* 6(4): 251–85.

College Board. 2014. *Institutional Methodology: Get the Full Picture*. https://secure-media.collegeboard.org/digitalServices/pdf/professionals/institutional-methodology.pdf, accessed 6/5/2020.

Collins, Benjamin. 2016. *Federal Student Aid: Need Analysis Formulas and Expected Family Contribution*. Washington, DC: Congressional Research Service. https://fas.org/sgp/crs/misc/R44503.pdf, accessed 6/5/2020.

Congressional Budget Office. 2020. *Income-Driven Repayment Plans for Student Loans: Budgetary Costs and Policy Options*. Washington, DC: Congressional Budget Office.

Cook, Emily E., and Sarah Turner. 2021. "Progressivity of Pricing at U.S. Public Universities." Tulane University Working Paper Series, Working Paper 2103.

Cooper, Preston. 2017. "If Higher Education Were a Public Good." *Forbes*, August 18. https://www.forbes.com/sites/prestoncooper2/2017/08/18/if-higher-education-were-a-public-good/#78e8ce433dc6, accessed 5/20/2020.

Crandall-Hollick, Margot L. 2018. *The American Opportunity Tax Credit: Overview, Analysis, and Policy Options*. Washington, DC: Congressional Research Service.

Dale, Stacy B., and Alan B. Krueger. 2014. "Estimating the Effects of College Characteristics over the Career Using Administrative Earnings Data." *Journal of Human Resources* 49(2):323–358.

Dann, Carrie. 2017. "Americans Split on Whether 4-Year College Degree Is Worth the Cost." NBC News. https://www.nbcnews.com/politics/first-read/americans -split-whether-4-year-college-degree-worth-cost-n799336, accessed 6/8/2020.

Dawson, Rachel Fulcher, Melissa S. Kearney, and James X. Sullivan. 2020. "Comprehensive Approaches to Increasing Student Completion in Higher Education: A Survey of the Landscape." NBER Working Paper 28046.

Debaun, Bill, and Carrie Warrick. 2019. *The Growing Gap: Public Higher Education's Declining Affordability for Low-Income Students.* Washington, DC: National College Attainment Network.

Deming, David, and Susan M. Dynarski. 2010. "College Aid." In *Targeting Investments in Children: Fighting Poverty When Resources Are Limited,* ed. Phillip B. Levine and David J. Zimmerman, 283–302. Chicago: National Bureau of Economic Research and University of Chicago Press.

Denning, Jeffrey T., Benjamin M. Marx, and Lesley J. Turner. 2019. "ProPelled: The Effects of Grants on Graduation, Earnings, and Welfare." *American Economic Journal: Applied Economics* 11(3): 193–224.

Depalma, Anthony. 1991. "Ivy Universities Deny Price-Fixing but Agree to Avoid It in the Future." *New York Times,* May 23. https://www.nytimes.com /1991/05/23/us/ivy-universities-deny-price-fixing-but-agree-to-avoid-it-in-the -future.html, accessed 5/20/2020.

Desrochers, Donna M., and Steven Hurlburt. 2016. *Trends in College Spending, 2003–2013: Where Does the Money Come From? Where Does It Go? What Does It Buy?* Washington, DC: American Institutes for Research.

Dynarski, Susan. 2016. The Trouble with Student Loans? Low Earnings, Not High Debt. Washington, DC: Brookings Institution.

Dynarski, Susan, C. J. Libassi, Katherine Michelmore, and Stephanie Owen. 2021. "Closing the Gap: The Effect of a Targeted, Tuition-Free Promise on College Choices of High-Achieving, Low-Income Students." *American Economic Review* 111(6): 1721–56.

Dynarski, Susan, and Judith Scott-Clayton. 2007. "College Grants on a Postcard: A Proposal for Simple and Predictable Federal Student Aid." Hamilton Project Discussion Paper 2007-01. Washington, DC: Brookings Institution.

———. 2013. "Financial Aid Policy: Lessons from Research." *Future of Children* 23: 67–91.

Education Commission of the States. 2020. *50-State Comparison: State Policies on Postsecondary Tuition Setting, Capping and Freezing.* https://www.ecs.org/50 -state-comparison-state-policies-on-postsecondary-tuition/, accessed 5/24/2020.

Epple, Dennis N., Richard Romano, Sinan Sarpca, Holger Sieg, and Melanie A. Zaber. 2019. "Market Power and Price Discrimination in the US Market for Higher Education." *RAND Journal of Economics* 50(1): 201–25.

Federal Reserve Bank of New York. 2020. *Quarterly Report on Household Debt and Credit 2020: Q2*. New York: Federal Reserve Bank of New York.

Finney, Joni. 2016. "College Unaffordable Even in Higher Income Brackets." *New York Times*, June 22.

Freedman, Josh. 2013. "How Not to Help the Poor: The Lesson of Soaring College Prices." *Atlantic*, July 10. https://www.theatlantic.com/business/archive/2013/07/how-not-to-help-the-poor-the-lesson-of-soaring-college-prices/277658/, accessed 8/16/2020.

Fuller, Matthew B. 2014. "A History of Financial Aid to Students." *Journal of Student Financial Aid* 44(1): article 4.

Goldrick-Rab, Sara. 2016. *Paying the Price: College Costs, Financial Aid, and the Betrayal of the American Dream*. Chicago: University of Chicago Press.

Goldrick-Rab, Sara, Robert Kelchen, Douglas N. Harris, and James Benson. 2016. "Reducing Income Inequality in Higher Education: Experimental Evidence on the Impact of Financial Aid on College Completion." *American Journal of Sociology* 121(6): 1762–1817.

Goolsbee, Austan, Steven Levitt, and Chad Syverson. 2020. *Microeconomics*. 3rd ed. New York: Worth.

Grawe, Nathan D. 2018. *Demographics and the Demand for Education*. Baltimore: Johns Hopkins University Press.

———. 2021. *The Agile College: How Institutions Successfully Navigate Demographic Changes*. Baltimore: Johns Hopkins University Press.

Gruber, Jonathan, and Benjamin D. Sommers. 2019. "The Affordable Care Act's Effects on Patients, Providers, and the Economy: What We've Learned So Far." *Journal of Policy Analysis and Management* 38(4): 1028–52.

Gurantz, Oded. 2020. "What Does Free Community College Buy? Early Impacts from the Oregon Promise." *Journal of Policy Analysis and Management* 39(1): 11–35.

Gurantz, Oded, Jessica Howell, Mike Hurwitz, Cassandra Larson, Matea Pender, and Brooke White. 2019. "Realizing Your College Potential? Impacts of College Board's RYCP Campaign on Postsecondary Enrollment." Annenberg School, Brown University, EdWorkingPapers.

Halberstam, David L. 1953. "College Board Meeting to Discuss Monro Plan." *Harvard Crimson*, October 22.

Hechinger, Fred M. 1987. "Rising College Costs: Harsh Prospect for Society." *New York Times*, September 8.

Heller, Donald E. 2013. *Does Federal Financial Aid Drive Up College Prices?* Washington, DC: American Council on Education.

Hendren, Nathaniel, and Ben Sprung-Keyser. 2020. "A Unified Welfare Analysis of Government Policies." *Quarterly Journal of Economics* 135(3): 1209–1318.

Hershbein, Brad, and Melissa S. Kearney. 2014. "Major Decisions: What Graduates Earn over Their Lifetimes." Brookings Institution, Hamilton Project. https://www.hamiltonproject.org/papers/major_decisions_what_graduates_earn_over_their_lifetimes, accessed 11/3/2020.

Hershbein, Brad, Melissa S. Kearney, and Luke W. Pardue. 2020. "College Attainment, Income Inequality, and Economic Security: A Simulation Exercise." *AEA: Papers and Proceedings* 110: 352–55.

Hesel, Richard A., Wayne Camara, and Steve Kappler. 2015. "Student Perceptions on Price, Aid, and Debt Provide an Extraordinary Opportunity for Colleges and Universities." *StudentPoll* 11(1).

Hesel, Richard A., and David C. Meade Jr. 2012. "A Majority of Students Rule Out Colleges Based on Sticker Price." *Student Poll* 9(1).

Hesel, Richard A., and Ryan C. Williams. 2010. "Students and Parents Making Judgments about College Costs without Complete Information." *Student Poll* 8(1).

Hess, Abigail. 2020. "How Student Debt Became a $1.6 Trillion Crisis." CNBC. https://www.cnbc.com/2020/06/12/how-student-debt-became-a-1point6 -trillion-crisis.html, accessed 8/10/2020.

Hill, Catharine Bond. 2019. "Should All College Admissions Become Need-Blind?" *Wall Street Journal*, March 17. https://www.wsj.com/articles/should-all -college-admissions-become-need-blind-11552874521, accessed 8/16/2020.

Hinrichs, Peter L. 2016. "Trends in Expenditures by US Colleges and Universities, 1987–2013." *Economic Commentary* (Federal Reserve Bank of Cleveland), 2016-10.

Holzer, Harry J., and Sandy Baum. 2017. *Making College Work: Pathways to Success for Disadvantaged Students*. Washington, DC: Brookings Institution Press.

Honan, William H. 1998. "Growing Gap Is Found in College Affordability and Grants to Needy Students." *New York Times*, November 18.

Horn, Laura J., Xianglei Chen, and Chris Chapman. 2003. *Getting Ready to Pay for College: What Students and Their Parents Know about the Cost of College Tuition and What They Are Doing to Find Out*. Washington, DC: National Center for Education Statistics, Institute of Education Sciences, US Department of Education.

Hoxby, Caroline M. 1998. "How Much Does School Spending Depend on Family Income? The Historical Origins of the Current School Finance Dilemma." *American Economic Review* 88(2): 309–14.

Hoxby, Caroline M., and C. Avery. 2013. "The Missing 'One-Offs': The Hidden Supply of High-Achieving, Low-Income Students." *Brookings Papers on Economic Activity*. 1: 1–65.

Hoxby, Caroline M., and Sarah Turner. 2013. "Expanding College Opportunities for High-Achieving, Low Income Students." SIEPR Discussion Paper 12-014. https://siepr.stanford.edu/sites/default/files/publications/12-014paper_6 .pdf.

———. 2015. "What High-Achieving Low-Income Students Know about College." *American Economic Review* 105(5): 514–17.

Ikenberry, Stanley O., and Terry W. Hartle. 1998. *Too Little Knowledge Is a Dangerous Thing: What the Public Thinks and Knows about Paying for College.* Washington, DC: American Council on Education.

Jaschik, Scott. 2019. "NACAC Agrees to Change Its Code of Ethics." *Inside Higher Education*, September 30. https://www.insidehighered.com/admissions /article/2019/09/30/nacac-agrees-change-its-code-ethics, accessed 5/20/2020.

Johnstone, D. Bruce. 2016. "Financing American Higher Education in the 21st Century: What Can the United States Learn from Other Countries?" Paper prepared for the National Commission on Financing 21st Century Higher Education. Charlottesville: University of Virginia, Miller Center.

Johnstone, D. Bruce, and Pamela N. Marcucci. 2010. *Financing Higher Education Worldwide: Who Pays? Who Should Pay?* Baltimore: Johns Hopkins University Press.

Kerr, Emma. 2019. "Is College Worth the Cost?" *U.S. News and World Report*, June 17. https://www.usnews.com/education/best-colleges/paying-for-college /articles/2019-06-17/is-college-worth-the-cost, accessed 6/9/2020.

Kim, E. Tammy. 2019. "What Free College Really Means." *New York Times*, June 30. https://www.nytimes.com/2019/06/30/opinion/warren-sanders-free-college .html, accessed 5/20/2020.

Kirkeboen, Lars J., Edwin Leuven, and Magne Mogstad. 2016. "Field of Study, Earnings, and Self-Selection." *Quarterly Journal of Economics* 131(3): 1057–1111.

Kirst, Seamus. 2019. "The Crippling Anxiety of Living with $100,000 in Student Loans." VICE. https://www.vice.com/en_au/article/mbdz4y/student-loans-anxiety -dating, accessed 8/10/2020.

Krupnick, Matt. 2020. "Students Who Counted on Work-Study Jobs Now Struggle to Pay Their Bills." *Washington Post*, October 22. https://www.washingtonpost .com/local/education/college-work-study-coronavirus/2020/10/21/e70c4f72 -131d-11eb-ba42-ec6a580836ed_story.html, accessed 11/19/2020.

Lafortune, Julien, Jesse Rothstein, and Diane Whitmore Schanzenbach. 2018. "School Finance Reform and the Distribution of Student Achievement." *American Economic Journal: Applied Economics* 10(2): 1–26.

Leonhardt, David. 2017. "America's Great Working-Class Colleges." *New York Times*, January 18. https://www.nytimes.com/2017/01/18/opinion/sunday/americas -great-working-class-colleges.html, accessed 8/22/2021.

Levesque, Elizabeth Mann. 2018. *Improving Community College Completion Rates by Addressing Structural and Motivational Barriers.* Washington, DC: Brookings Institution. https://www.brookings.edu/research/community-college-completion -rates-structural-and-motivational-barriers, accessed 5/14/2020.

Levine, Phillip B. 2014. *Transparency in College Costs.* Brookings Institution, Economic Studies Working Paper, November. https://www.brookings.edu/wp -content/uploads/2016/06/12_transparency_in_college_costs_levine.pdf, accessed 5/28/2020.

Levine, Phillip B., Jennifer Ma, and Lauren Russell. 2020. "Do College Applicants Respond to Changes in Sticker Prices Even When They Don't Matter?" National Bureau of Economic Research Working Paper 26910. https://www.nber.org/papers/w26910.

Lewin, Tamar. 2008. "College May Become Unaffordable for Most in U.S." *New York Times*, December 3.

Lochner, Lance, and Alexander Monge-Naranjo. 2012. *Annual Review of Economics* 4: 225–56.

Looney, Adam. 2020. "Dept. of Education's College Scorecard Shows Where Student Loans Pay Off . . . and Where They Don't." Washington, DC: Brookings Institution. https://www.brookings.edu/research/ed-depts-college-scorecard-shows-where-student-loans-pay-off-and-where-they-dont/, accessed 11/23/2020.

Looney, Adam, and Constantine Yannelis. 2015. "A Crisis in Student Loans? How Changes in the Characteristics of Borrowers and in the Institutions They Attended Contributed to Rising Loan Defaults." *Brookings Papers on Economic Activity*, Fall.

Ma, Jennifer, Matea Pender, and C. J. Libassi. 2020. *Trends in College Pricing and Financial Aid 2020*. Washington, DC: College Board.

Mahan, Shannon M. 2011. *Federal Pell Grant Program of the Higher Education Act: Background, Recent Changes, and Current Legislative Issues*. Washington, DC: Congressional Research Service.

Mankiw, N. Gregory. 2021. *Principles of Microeconomics*. 9th ed. Boston: Cengage.

Marcotte, Dave E. 2019. "The Returns to Education at Community Colleges: New Evidence from the Education Longitudinal Survey." *Education Finance and Policy* 14(4): 523–47.

Markin, Stephanie. 2020. *About a Quarter of U.S. Adults Consider Higher Ed Affordable*. Washington, DC: Gallup.

McFarland, J., B. Hussar, J. Zhang, X. Wang, K. Wang, S. Hein, M. Diliberti, E. Forrest Cataldi, F. Bullock Mann, and A. Barmer. 2019. *The Condition of Education, 2019*. NCES 2019-144. Washington, DC: National Center for Education Statistics, Institute of Education Sciences, US Department of Education.

McPherson, Michael S., and Morton Owen Schapiro. 1998. *The Student Aid Game: Meeting Need and Rewarding Talent in American Higher Education*. Princeton, NJ: Princeton University Press.

Moretti, Enrico. 2004. "Estimating the Social Return to Higher Education: Evidence from Longitudinal and Repeated Cross-Sectional Data." *Journal of Econometrics* 121: 175–212.

Mulhere, Kaitlin. 2019. "These 75 Colleges Promise to Meet 100% of Students' Financial Need." *Money*. https://money.com/colleges-that-meet-full-financial-need/, accessed 4/16/2020.

NACUBO-TIAA. 2020. *2019 NACUBO-TIAA Study of Endowments*. Washington, DC: NACUBO.

NASFAA Policy & Federal Relations Staff. 2021. "ASFAA Deep Dive: Changes to Federal Methodology, Other Student Aid Changes From Spending Bill." https://www.nasfaa.org/news-item/24269/NASFAA_Deep-Dive_Changes_to_Federal_Methodology_Other_Student_Aid_Changes_From_Spending_Bill.

Nash, Margaret A. 2019. "Entangled Pasts: Land-Grant Colleges and American Indian Dispossession." *History of Education Quarterly* 59(4): 437–67.

National Association of Student Financial Aid Administrators. 2014. Need Analysis Participant Handout. Washington, DC: National Association of Student Financial Aid Administrators. https://www.kasfaa.com/pdf/NASFAA2014Work shop.pdf, accessed 11/6/2020.

National Postsecondary Education Cooperative. 2009. *Information Required to Be Disclosed under the Higher Education Act of 1965: Suggestions for Dissemination (Updated)*. NPEC 2010-831v2, prepared by Carol Fuller and Carlo Salerno, Coffey Consulting. Washington, DC.

Nguyen, Tuan D., Jenna W. Kramer, and Brent J. Evans. 2019. "The Effects of Grant Aid on Student Persistence and Degree Completion: A Systematic Review and Meta-Analysis of the Causal Evidence." *Review of Educational Research* 89(6): 831–74.

Oreopoulos, Philip, and Uros Petronijevic. 2013. "Making College Worth It: A Review of the Returns to Higher Education." *Future of Children* 23(1): 41–66.

Page, Lindsay C., Stacy S. Kehoe, Benjamin L. Castleman, and Gumilang Aryo Sahadewo. 2019. "More Than Dollars for Scholars: The Impact of the Dell Scholars Program on College Access, Persistence, and Degree Attainment." *Journal of Human Resources* 43(3): 683–725.

Page, Lindsay C., and Judith Scott-Clayton. 2016. "Improving College Access in the United States: Barriers and Policy Responses." *Economics of Education Review* 51: 4–22.

Pallais, Amanda. 2015. "Small Differences That Matter: Mistakes in Applying to College." *Journal of Labor Economics* 33(2): 493–520.

Perna, L. W., J. Wright-Kim, and N. Jiang. 2019. *Questioning the Calculations: Are Colleges Complying with Federal and Ethical Mandates for Providing Students with Estimated Costs?* Penn AHEAD Research Brief—March 2019. Philadelphia: Alliance for Higher Education and Democracy (Penn AHEAD), University of Pennsylvania Graduate School of Education.

Peterson, Iver. 1973. "College Costs Will Rise Sharply Again Next Fall." *New York Times*, May 3.

Powell, Farran, and Emma Kerr. 2020. "Schools That Meet Full Financial Need with No Loans." *US News and World Report*, September 24.

Reed, Matthew, and Robert Shireman. 2008. *Time to Reexamine Institutional Cooperation on Financial Aid*. Berkeley, CA: Institute for College Access and Success.

Salop, Steven C., and Lawrence J. White. 1991. "Policy Watch: Antitrust Goes to College." *Journal of Economic Perspectives* 5(3): 193–202.

Schemo, Diana Jean. 2001. "Cost of Tuition and Other College Fees Go Up." *New York Times*, October 24.

Shapiro, Doug, Afet Dundar, Faye Huie, Phoebe Wakhungu, Xin Yuan, Angel Nathan, and Youngsik Hwang. 2017. *Tracking Transfer: Measures of Effectiveness in Helping Community College Students to Complete Bachelor's Degrees.* Signature Report 13. Herndon, VA: National Student Clearinghouse Research Center.

Smith, Jonathan, Joshua Goodman, and Michael Hurwitz. 2020. "The Economic Impact of Access to Public Four-Year Colleges." NBER Working Paper 27177.

Snyder, Thomas D., Cristobal de Brey, and Sally A. Dillow. 2019. *Digest of Education Statistics 2018.* NCES 2020-009. Washington, DC: National Center for Education Statistics, Institute of Education Sciences, US Department of Education.

The Institute for College Access and Success. 2012. *Adding It All Up: Are College Net Price Calculators Easy to Find, Use, and Compare?* Washington, DC: Institute for College Access and Success.

———. 2017. *Cost in Translation: How Financial Aid Award Letters Fall Short.* Oakland, CA: Institute for College Access and Success. https://ticas.org/wp-content/uploads/legacy-files/pub_files/cost_in_translation.pdf, accessed 8/12/2020.

Thelin, John R. 2011. *A History of American Higher Education.* Baltimore: Johns Hopkins University Press.

Tough, Paul. 2019. *The Years That Matter Most: How College Makes Us or Breaks Us.* New York: Houghton Mifflin Harcourt.

Turner, Lesley. 2020. "The Economic Incidence of Federal Student Grant Aid." Unpublished manuscript, Vanderbilt University.

Turner, Sarah. 2018. "The Evolution of the High Tuition, High Aid Debate." *Change* 50(3–4): 142–48.

US Bureau of Labor Statistics. 2020. *Usual Weekly Earnings of Wage and Salary Workers, First Quarter 2020.* Washington, DC: Bureau of Labor Statistics. https://www.bls.gov/news.release/pdf/wkyeng.pdf, accessed 6/8/2020.

Velez, Erin Dunlop, and Laura Horn. 2018. *What High Schoolers and Their Parents Know about Public 4-Year Tuition and Fees in Their State.* Washington, DC: National Center for Education Statistics, Institute of Education Sciences, US Department of Education.

Warner, John. 2019. "The Return of Hope: Thinking about a Future of Higher Ed as a Public Good." *Inside Higher Ed*, May 1. https://www.insidehighered.com/blogs/just-visiting/return-hope-thinking-about-future-higher-ed-public-good, accessed 5/20/2020.

White House, Office of the Press Secretary. 2015. FACT SHEET: The President's Plan for Early Financial Aid: Improving College Choice and Helping More Americans Pay for College. https://obamawhitehouse.archives.gov/the-press-office/2015/09/14/fact-sheet-president%E2%80%99s-plan-early-financial-aid-improving-college-choice, accessed 11/6/2020.

Wilkinson, Rupert. 2005. *Aiding Students, Buying Students: Financial Aid in America*. Nashville: Vanderbilt University Press.

Zimmerman, Seth D. 2014. "The Returns to College Admission for Academically Marginal Students." *Journal of Labor Economics* 32(4): 711–54.

Zinth, K., and M. Smith. 2012. "Tuition-Setting Authority for Public Colleges and Universities." Education Commission of the States. https://www.ecs.org/clearing house/01/04/71/10471.pdf, accessed 4/20/20.

Index

The letter *f* following a page number denotes a figure and the letter *t* following denotes a table.